Lecture Notes in Computer Science

Lecture Notes in Artificial Intelligence 14377

Founding Editor

Jörg Siekmann

AF790404

Series Editors

Randy Goebel, *University of Alberta, Edmonton, AB, Canada*
Wolfgang Wahlster, *DFKI, Berlin, Germany*
Zhi-Hua Zhou, *Nanjing University, Nanjing, China*

The series Lecture Notes in Artificial Intelligence (LNAI) was established in 1988 as a topical subseries of LNCS devoted to artificial intelligence.

The series publishes state-of-the-art research results at a high level. As with the LNCS mother series, the mission of the series is to serve the international R & D community by providing an invaluable service, mainly focused on the publication of conference and workshop proceedings and postproceedings.

David Restrepo Amariles · Ken Satoh
Editors

Compliance for Artificial Intelligence Systems

Strategies, Principles and Methods

Springer

Editors
David Restrepo Amariles
HEC Paris
Jouy-en-Josas, France

Ken Satoh
Center for Juris-Informatics, ROIS-DS
Tokyo, Japan

ISSN 0302-9743 ISSN 1611-3349 (electronic)
Lecture Notes in Artificial Intelligence
ISBN 978-3-032-12794-5 ISBN 978-3-032-12795-2 (eBook)
https://doi.org/10.1007/978-3-032-12795-2

LNCS Sublibrary: SL7 – Artificial Intelligence

© The Editor(s) (if applicable) and The Author(s), under exclusive license
to Springer Nature Switzerland AG 2026

This work is subject to copyright. All rights are solely and exclusively licensed by the Publisher, whether the whole or part of the material is concerned, specifically the rights of translation, reprinting, reuse of illustrations, recitation, broadcasting, reproduction on microfilms or in any other physical way, and transmission or information storage and retrieval, electronic adaptation, computer software, or by similar or dissimilar methodology now known or hereafter developed.
The use of general descriptive names, registered names, trademarks, service marks, etc. in this publication does not imply, even in the absence of a specific statement, that such names are exempt from the relevant protective laws and regulations and therefore free for general use.
The publisher, the authors and the editors are safe to assume that the advice and information in this book are believed to be true and accurate at the date of publication. Neither the publisher nor the authors or the editors give a warranty, expressed or implied, with respect to the material contained herein or for any errors or omissions that may have been made. The publisher remains neutral with regard to jurisdictional claims in published maps and institutional affiliations.

This Springer imprint is published by the registered company Springer Nature Switzerland AG
The registered company address is: Gewerbestrasse 11, 6330 Cham, Switzerland

If disposing of this product, please recycle the paper.

Preface

The recent development of AI technologies — especially large language models and new autonomous agents — and their accelerating adoption by public and private organizations have made compliance a key concern for both operators and regulators. As AI systems increasingly mediate critical functions in economic, legal, and social domains, their deployment must be guided not only by technical robustness but also by comprehensive frameworks of accountability, legality, and ethical responsibility. At the same time, regulatory approaches are diverging significantly across jurisdictions. The European Union has taken the lead with a risk-based model embedded in the AI Act, which emphasizes trustworthiness, the protection of fundamental rights, and human oversight. In contrast, the United States has largely relied on the National Institute of Standards and Technology (NIST) to issue non-binding guidance, technical standards, and support for industry-led self-regulation. Japan has adopted a facilitative approach, promoting innovation and adoption while deliberately avoiding top-down regulatory intervention. In other parts of the world, more fragmented or market-driven governance models are emerging. In this complex and evolving landscape, compliance has become a critical mechanism through which organizations can reconcile varying regulatory demands, ensure the safe and responsible deployment of AI systems, and manage legal, ethical, and operational risks in a systematic and transparent manner.

This state-of-the-art survey brings together interdisciplinary contributions that reflect the plurality of methods, principles, and strategies needed to address the complex challenge of AI compliance. It aims to provide both conceptual grounding and practical tools to support the development, evaluation, and governance of AI systems that are not only functional but also lawful.

Several articles in this volume demonstrate the importance of bridging technical and legal disciplines. For example, Meloche et al. propose a web-based environment for the specification and automated monitoring of smart legal contracts, advancing formal methods to ensure contract compliance in complex, dynamic environments such as transactive energy markets. Gyory et al. introduce GDPR120Q, a large-scale annotated dataset designed to support compliance with European data protection law through legal natural language processing techniques, illustrating how benchmark datasets can enable scalable, explainable compliance verification. Bhambhoria et al. argue for open-source legal AI systems as a way to ensure transparency, reduce hallucinations, and promote fairness in access to legal assistance, thus responding to the structural limitations of general-purpose large language models in sensitive legal tasks.

Other contributions in this book explore the normative and epistemic dimensions of AI compliance. Charlotin reflects on the role of variance in legal decision — making — both human and algorithmic — and whether AI systems should replicate or suppress such variability to maintain the integrity of law. Dalla Giovanna et al. examine how current university curricula in computer science fail to adequately prepare future AI developers for the ethical and legal obligations imposed by emerging regulations such as the AI Act, revealing a critical gap in the formation of compliance — oriented professionals. Finally, Yang et al. explore the issue of shadow adoption of AI, along with the organizational and regulatory implications of disclosing the use of generative AI tools in professional environments. They demonstrate how agency dynamics and information asymmetries generate risks in the workplace adoption of generative AI systems and they outline key elements that corporate AI policies should incorporate to promote responsible use.

Taken together, these contributions advance the proposition that AI compliance is a multi-dimensional, cross-disciplinary effort. It requires operational tools, legal awareness, and institutional safeguards. Importantly, this volume underscores that compliance cannot be reduced to a mere checklist of technical specifications or legal formalities. Rather, it must be understood as a dynamic and ongoing process of aligning the design and deployment of AI systems with organizational values, societal norms, and evolving regulatory expectations.

By bringing together perspectives from computer science, law, and organizational practice, this book offers a foundational contribution to the growing literature on compliance of AI systems, and it underscores the need for co-production of AI governance among technologists, lawyers, regulators, and users. We thank for reviewers for this volume, Charlotte Alexander, Karim Benyekhlef, Peter Fratrič, Randy Goebel, Raphaël Gyory, Nils Holzenberger, Gregory Lewkowicz, Yoshiaki Nishigai, and Katsumi Nitta. We hope that readers will find these works both intellectually stimulating and practically useful as they confront the challenge of building safe, lawful, and trustworthy AI systems.

October 1, 2025

David Restrepo Amariles
Ken Satoh

Contents

Formalised Legal Principles in Rule-Based Artificial Intelligence

David Fernández-Duque and Joost J. Joosten(✉)

University of Barcelona, Barcelona, Spain
jjoosten@ub.edu

Abstract. We study Rule-based Artificial Intelligence in the legal sector. We wish to see how various legal principles can be warranted in, for example, automated law enforcement. We observe that dialogues with algorithms could be an important step to safeguarding legal principles for legal software. Moreover, we observe that dialogues are often possible once formal methods are used. Dialogues with software cannot guarantee all legal principles. As an example we mention Transparency and Legal Certainty. These principles are then compared to each other in the realm of algorithmic law. Computational hurdles imply a clear separation of these two principles.

Keywords: Legal Software · Formal Methods · Legal Principles · Human in the Loop

1 Introduction

Artificial Intelligence (AI) is growing more present in our society by the day. In particular, AI is also increasingly applied to the legal field. Automated decision making and automated law enforcement are just some examples of that. It is paramount that AI in the legal sector does not violate rights of citizens. In this paper we will see how certain AI in the legal sector interacts with the fundamentals of proper legal practice as embodied by the basic Legal Principles like Justice, Equality, Legal Certainty, and Transparency to mention a few.

We make a novel but very simple observation that so far has never been made explicit: the use of formal methods can enable rudimentary forms of dialogues with algorithms. In particular, algorithms can be asked about their compliance with legal principles. In the first part of the paper we will see how this would work for two kinds of formal methods and as such it is largely based on the technical unpublished note *Dialogues with Algorithms* [1].

We will see that certain legal principles like Equality will benefit from dialogues with algorithms. However, not all legal principles can be warranted by

This research has been supported by project PID2023-151396OB-I00 of the Spanish Ministry of Science, Innovation and Universities and by 2022 DI 051 of the Generalitat de Catalunya.

© The Author(s), under exclusive license to Springer Nature Switzerland AG 2026
D. Restrepo Amariles and K. Satoh (Eds.): *Compliance for Artificial Intelligence Systems*, LNAI 14377, pp. 1–10, 2026.
https://doi.org/10.1007/978-3-032-12795-2_1

dialogues. As examples we mention the principles of Legal Certainty and of Transparency. Moreover, we will observe that those principles, though clearly related are substantially different.

We would like to stress that our approach is based on formal methods and as such we aim at mathematical certainty in attesting that the algorithms behave according to various legal principles. Of course, any legal software is designed aiming to be fair, just, treating equal data sets with equal outcomes, etc. But in regular programming these properties are typically only *tested* for during the lifecycle of the software so that full certainty can typically not be attained. Recent developments sketch how even Generative AI based on Large Language Models can be used for so-called meta-reasoning and property-based testing [2].[1] Thus, our proposed strategy sets itself apart[2] through the use of formal methods to prove compliance with (formalisations of) legal principles. To the best of our knowledge this has not yet been thoroughly carried out in the literature.

2 Legal Principles and Human in the Loop

It is commonly held that during automated legal decision making there should be human oversight and involvement. As a matter of fact, the human involvement is anchored in various legal instruments most notably in the European GDPR [4], quoting from Article 22.1:

> The data subject shall have the right not to be subject to a decision based solely on automated processing, including profiling, which produces legal effects concerning him or her or similarly significantly affects him or her.

The more recent EU AI Act [5] dedicates an entire article to human oversight; quoting from Article 14.1 (Human oversight):

> High-risk AI systems shall be designed and developed in such a way, including with appropriate human-machine interface tools, that they can be effectively overseen by natural persons during the period in which the AI system is in use.

However, it is far from clear what such human involvement should look like. Some argue that often, having a human in the loop is considered unjustly as a magic potion to warrant correct decisions but that human oversight in general falls short as a solution to the risks of algorithmic decision-making [6]. Notwithstanding, all scholars agree that some degree of human oversight and involvement is needed though, again, there is no common notion of what this should look like (see also [7]).

Human overview should minimise or mitigate undesired effects of using AI and automated decision making like biases/discrimination, nudging, opaqueness or simply errors [8–10]. In more general terms, human oversight should warrant that the basic legal principles are respected by the AI applications.

[1] We are grateful to one of the reviewers to point out to us this most relevant paper.

[2] Another mention of formal methods and legal principles is in [3].

An important parameter in the discussion on correct human involvement in legal automated decision making is the kind of AI that is used. For example, transparency in Neural Networks is much harder to achieve (if not impossible) than in old-style rule based AI [11]. In this paper we shall therefore focus on Rule based AI since, as we shall see, recent development of formal methods can facilitate certain rudimentary forms of dialogues with and interrogations of algorithms on how they perform and what kind of properties these algorithms have [12]. In particular, such dialogues can allow to check for compliance with some legal principles.

3 Black-Boxes and Dialogues

We decide to focus on classical legal computer programs in this paper leaving other paradigms like neural networks and the like aside. Thus, we focus on programs that follow our human ideal logical reasoning schemes in an algorithmic fashion. The resulting legal computer programs often leads to problems. Users or those affected may object to legal software and claim to lose transparency, oversight, understanding and fear errors. As a matter of fact, all substantially large computer programs do contain errors, be they typos, small design errors, or programmed biases (see [12]). However, all these objections also hold for human actors in the law enforcement who also err, have personal inclinations and preferences and may be methodologically far from optimal.

An essential difference between legal computer programs and human legal actors lies in the possibility to *dialogue*. For example, with a human legal actor there is less fear of loss of transparency. For sure, the legal actor may and most likely will be much more knowledgeable than us, but at least we have the feeling that we can pose questions, ask explanations, and inquire for the basic assumptions. Those acts of interaction are at least cumbersome with a program and not accessible to the average citizen. In various known cases of erroneous software in the past we see that interaction took very long, and over sometimes years went through various committees and groups of experts.

A notorious example is the Dutch SyRI social risk scoring computer algorithm [13]. SyRI would assign a fraud risk score to citizens on the basis of which social support could be denied. Only after years of allegations and human tragedy of involved individuals it was shown and understood that the algorithm was biased and, for example, would not act equally on citizens that have more than one nationality. We imagine the amount of tragedy and time that could have been saved if at an early stage, one could have asked the program how it functioned. For example, imagine that x and y range over data containers for individual citizens. And imagine that $\mathcal{A}$ is the set of all attributes[3] of those citizens, that $\mathsf{NrOfPassports}(z)$ is a function that tells how many different passports (nationalities) an individual z possesses and that $\mathsf{Score}(z)$ is the score that individual z

[3] For the sake of exposition we restrict to unary attributes, like "z is female" but the example can easily be extended to relations of higher arity.

obtains by the SyRI algorithm. We can then formalise the question of whether SyRi would be biased for multiple passport holders:

$$\forall x, y \Big((\mathsf{NrOfPassports}(x) \neq \mathsf{NrOfPassports}(y)) \wedge \bigwedge_{P \in \mathcal{A}} (P(x) \leftrightarrow P(y)) \Longrightarrow \mathsf{Score}(x) = \mathsf{Score}(y) \Big)$$

Clearly, this is a property that either holds true or false of the SyRI software. In a sense the property reflects an important manifestation of the legal principle of Equality. If only citizens would have been able at an early stage to query this question to the program, it is likely that the whole affair would have been less painful and time-consuming.

The SyRI software was designed and gauged using external data that was statistically analysed. The exact choices made during this gauging and statistical analysis are important for society but are not reflected in the program itself. Nonetheless, the behaviour of the program can in principle be queried agains properties like the one formalised here above. In general, one can imagine that enabling dialogues with programs could restore trust and control in the interaction between human actors and software.

We wish to stress that merely having access to the source code of a legal program is a necessary but not a sufficient condition to guarantee Legal Certainty. In Sect. 5 below we shall come back to this. Even for IT specialists it is extremely hard to fully understand the exact working of computer code. As a matter of fact in its full generality, full understanding of the source code is impossible since it would imply that we can solve the unsolvable Halting Problem.

Regarding Legal Certainty, it seems like a bare minimum to at least grant access to the source code so that citizens that are affected by the functioning of that code may try to understand how the code works. In this regard it is curious to mention the BOSCO case in Spain. BOSCO is a state owned computer program that decides who qualifies for social financial support. Supposedly, BOSCO follows a fully determined legal text but numerous wrong decisions made by the program have been reported [14]. Notwithstanding supported claims of errors, Spanish administration is still reluctant to disclose the software. This is to be contrasted with French practice and regulation [15], where they strive for open software in public administrations.

Ponce-Solé points out in [16] that Article 9.3 of the Spanish Constitution prohibits arbitrariness in legal decision making. The very same article however also mentions that norms should be publicly announced. This begs the discussion that if the implementation of the law fills in substantial blanks in that law or reinterprets a law, if it then should be allowed for this implementation to be proprietary or to remain undisclosed. Note that filling blanks or reinterpreting is typically needed to go from natural language to executable code.

Through the examples above, we think it is convincingly showcased that when there is no access to nor precise understanding of the source code, Transparency is at stake and it will become extremely hard for citizens to contest automated decisions that concern their rights.

4 Formal Methods Enable Dialogues

Engaging in a dialogue with a software program may sound extremely futuristic. In a rudimentary form, however, this is possible and almost already in place. However, it can only be applied in the case the software is embedded in an environment of formal methods like software correctness proofs or model checking.

Formal methods refers to a large collection of techniques where mathematics and logic is employed to reason about, most prominently, the correctness of algorithms/software. As we have seen, correctness/robustness is of utmost importance and currently receives much attention. Robustness is discussed in the European AI Act (e.g. [5], Article 15) and it seems that the only way to achieve a serious level of robustness is by employing formal methods. Often, the use of formal methods implicitly opens the door to enabling rudimentary dialogues with software. We shall discuss this for two paradigms: model checking and software synthesis through proof assistants. Let us start with the latter.

Proof assistants typically check mathematical proofs for correctness. One may think, aren't mathematical proofs by definition correct? The answer is no. That is to say, most proofs will contain minor errors though oftentimes these errors can easily be repaired by slightly tweaking the argument. Sometimes, mathematicians don't even see the small error since it is clear how the global logical structure of the argument goes. Another 'error' could be the omission of an easy reasoning step. Proof assistants like Coq, Isabelle or Lean, to mention only a few, are small computer programs that perform a simple task. When they are presented with a mathematical proof, they will check step by step that each alleged larger-scale reasoning indeed has a proof. Using proof assistants in mathematics has lead to various new insights, a few new theorems and numerous detections of flaws in proofs [17].

If the language of a proof assistant is rich enough, one can express software in it and moreover, one can express substantial software *behaviour* in it. Thus, in the environment of a proof assistant, one can make claims about the software. We call this a formal specification when the claims fully describe the desired behaviour of the software. Consequently, once a piece of software lives inside a proof assistant environment, this automatically enables questions to be posed about the software and behold our dialogue. The caveat here is that it will be the programmer/user of the proof assistant who will need to provide a formally verified answer to the question. This means answering the question and proving that the answer is indeed correct. This feels like falling short as a real dialogue but at least certainty about the answers will be obtained (provided we accept that the very small proof assistant program itself is correct). Moreover, very few software is being obtained through the use of proof assistants, let alone legal software. In this context we mention a project to formalise European (freight) traffic regulation software inside Coq that has resulted so far to a formally verified time library [18].

Within model checking in law, it seems that dialogues may come somewhat easier. A legal model checking paradigm is described in [19] and would run as follows. In this paradigm, a computable law would be expressed as a formula φ

in some formal language $\mathcal{L}$ that is rich enough to express the law under consideration. Next, we consider data files that describe particular cases to which the law should be tested. The data files are formally viewed as mathematical structures often called model. Thus, we can consider each data file as a model $\mathcal{M}$ and a different data file gives rise to a (typically) different model. If we wish to inquire if the case $\mathcal{M}$ is legal or not according to the law φ we resort to techniques of model checking and the question will boil down to

$$\mathcal{M} \models \varphi \, ?$$

Thus, given a model $\mathcal{M}$ and a formula φ, does the model $\mathcal{M}$ make true the formula φ yes or no? We should stress here that this question in general need not be decidable (recall the Halting Problem). Or if it is decidable, it may not be feasible. The art in legal model checking thus resides in choosing the language $\mathcal{L}$ rich enough so that various interesting laws can be expressed in it. On the other hand, the language should not be too rich as to prevent undecidability or unfeasibility to kick in. Once such a balance is found, there are certain benefits of model checking over proof assistants: the same model-checking framework will work for a whole class of laws, whereas just minor tweaks in legal formally verified software may imply enormous tasks for the programmer to generate new proofs.

Of course, a model checker does not directly yield error free software since the implementation may still contain errors. An optimal situation seems to arise if the model checking algorithm is implemented using proof assistants but let us leave this matter aside here.

One can also consider the *consistency question*: is the law φ consistent, that is, is there some situation/model $\mathcal{M}$ that abides by the law, that is, is there some $\mathcal{M}$ so that $\mathcal{M} \models \varphi$? Directly related to the consistency question is the *tautology question*: is the law φ true in all possible situations/models? We use the standard notation

$$\models \varphi$$

for the tautology statement: φ holds true on all models $\mathcal{M}$. In our setting this is tantamount to saying that the law φ is satisfied in every possible situation $\mathcal{M}$. It must be observed that the question $\models \varphi$ looks more complicated than $\mathcal{M} \models \varphi$ for a particular model. In general, this holds true and the tautology question is really harder (where the notion of harder being strictly harder often depends on complexity questions like $\mathsf{P} = \mathsf{NP}$) than just the model checking question. Notwithstanding, for various logics, like Linear Temporal Logic, the corresponding tautology question is decidable with not too bad computational properties.

Using the tautology question we can now enter in dialogue with the law as long as the dialogue is restricted to the linguistic fragment $\mathcal{L}$. Let ψ be some property that can be expressed in $\mathcal{L}$. The question of whether applying the law φ necessarily leads to having the property ψ can thus be stated as

$$\models \varphi \to \psi.$$

We observe the difference in both paradigms: in the proof assistant environment we could directly ask questions about the software. However, these questions were to be replied and proven by the user itself. In the model checking environment, we can pose questions about the law φ. In this case, however, the questions are automatically answered by the model (tautology) checking algorithm. One can argue that a formalisation φ of a computable law can actually be seen as a program. Up to now, laws are typically written in natural languages and a formalisation φ in a logic $\mathcal{L}$ can be seen as a program: a translation of a written computable law into a particular model of computation with the formal specification being quite similar to a program.

5 Legal Certainty Versus Transparency

So far we have seen how formal methods enable rudimentary dialogues with software. In particular, in Sect. 3 we saw an example how instantiations of the principle of Equality could be expressed once a dialogue is enabled in a sufficiently expressible language. However, not all legal principles benefit from a mere dialogue with the software.

The Principle of Transparency is about access to information. Citizens should be entitled to access documents by the institutions and decision-making processes should be disclosed and public. Clearly, in our context, Transparency is not so much about the behaviour of the software but more about how it is disclosed. As such, a dialogue with the software will not directly improve transparency.

Closely related to Transparency is the principle of Legal Certainty. Roughly, Legal Certainty is understood as the requirement that those subject to a law must be able to foresee the legal consequences of their actions. In general, good access to the written law is a prerequisite for Legal Certainty. However, it is not sufficient to merely have access to the written law. Let us take an extreme and artificial example.

For our artificial example we use the Halting Problem. If a program Π halts on input A we will write $\Pi(A)\downarrow$ (we don't care about the output or what the program has done, and are just interested if it halted here). Turing proved that it is algorithmically unsolvable to decide whether for arbitrary Π and A we have $\Pi(A)\downarrow$. There is even a universal program U so that it is algorithmically unsolvable whether for arbitrary input A we have $U(A)\downarrow$. In the example below, let $D(t)$ denote the date-stamp of a given moment in time. Thus, $D(t)$ is some fixed numerical representation of a date. For example, in UNIX time it would be the number of seconds elapsed since the very start of 1970 until the current moment t. We now consider the following artificial law λ:

λ: Your behaviour wrt λ is legal at time t unless $U(D(t))\downarrow$.

Clearly, as long as we correctly publish λ, there is no problem as to Transparency. However, due to the general unsolvability of the Halting Problem we do not have Legal Certainty since in general it is principally unknowable[4] whether $U(A)\downarrow$.

Of course, our law λ is silly and artificial but there is a gradual sliding slope that takes us down to actual laws currently in force. As a next step we borrow an example from [20].

> Upon matrimonial divorce, each item in the common patrimony should be assigned a € amount and then the patrimony should be split between the partners in such a way that causes the minimal € difference in the division of goods between the partners.

The stipulation looks innocuous but again, Legal Certainty cannot be warranted. Imagine a marriage with a common patrimony of 1000 items. To comply with the law one would have to evaluate all 2^{1000} possible distributions of the items over the two partners. We know that this is a task impossible to perform once we realise that scientists estimate that there are around 10^{100} elementary particles in the visible universe. Various more examples are given in [19,20] of Legal Certainty at stake due to the complexity of the laws.

It is clear that in the case of algorithmic law, disclosure of the code is a prerequisite. Again, Transparency is a necessary condition for Legal Certainty. Especially in the case of algorithmic law, having access to the code is not a sufficient condition though to ensure Legal Certainty. As we have seen, code can have incomprehensible and unpredictable behaviour. And even if in principle the code is predictable, it may simply need too many resources to cast a reliable prediction. Legal Certainty for algorithmic law seems thus to require a relatively tame behaviour of the software that implements the law. Preliminary observations about such tame behaviour in terms of model-checking are presented in [19]. However, much work is still to be done in this direction. But given the civil rights at stake it seems an inevitable road to walk.

6 Conclusion

We have seen two cases where the mere use of formal methods automatically enables a rudimentary form of dialogue between a program and the user of that program. The possibility of a dialogue is a main feature that sets human actors apart from automated actors in legal decision making. Dialogues can, in particular be used to inquire the software about its compliance with various legal principles of which we have seen some examples. We closed off by observing that *Certainty* and *Transparency* are trivially separated via for example, the Halting Problem or any computational problem that requires astronomically large computational resources.

[4] Of course, the prosecutor will have an equally hard time in this situation.

References

1. Joosten, J.J.: Dialogues with algorithms. arXiv preprint arXiv:2309.10678 (2023)
2. Padhye, R.: Software engineering methods for AI-driven deductive legal reasoning. arXiv preprint arXiv:2404.09868 (2024)
3. Le Métayer, D.: Formal methods as a link between software code and legal rules. In: Barthe, G., Pardo, A., Schneider, G. (eds.) Software Engineering and Formal Methods. SEFM 2011. LNCS, vol. 7041. Springer, Berlin, Heidelberg (2011)
4. Regulation (EU) 2016/679 of the European Parliament and of the Council of 27 April 2016 on the protection of natural persons with regard to the processing of personal data and on the free movement of such data, and repealing Directive 95/46/EC (General Data Protection Regulation)
5. Proposal for a Regulation of the European Parliament and of the Council Laying Down Harmonised Rules on Artificial Intelligence (Artificial Intelligence Act) and Amending Certain Union Legislative Acts, COM/2021/206 final
6. Green, B., Kak, A.: The false comfort of human oversight as an antidote to A.I. harm; slate (2021). https://slate.com/technology/2021/06/human-oversight-artificial-intelligence-laws.html
7. Portela, M., álvarez, T.: Towards a meaningful human oversight of automated decision-making systems. Digital Future Society (2022). https://digitalfuturesociety.com/report/towards-a-meaningful-human-oversight-of-automated-decision-making-systems/
8. Weerts, H., Xenidis, R., Tarissan, F., Olsen, H.P., Pechenizkiy, M.: Algorithmic unfairness through the lens of EU non-discrimination law: or why the law is not a decision tree. In: Proceedings of the 2023 ACM Conference on Fairness, Accountability, and Transparency (FAccT '23) (2023)
9. Schwartz, R., Vassilev, A., Greene, K., Perine, L., Burt, A., Hall, P.: Towards a standard for identifying and managing bias in artificial intelligence (NIST Special Publication 1270) (2022)
10. Yeung, K.: Algorithmic regulation: a critical interrogation. Regul. Governance **12**(4), 505–523 (2017)
11. Wiklicky, H.: The neural network loading problem is undecidable. In: Proceedings of the First European Conference on Computational Learning Theory, pp. 183 – 192. Oxford University Press (1994)
12. O'Regan, G.: Concise Guide to Formal Methods: Theory, Fundamentals and Industry Applications. Springer (2017)
13. SyRI legislation in breach of European Convention on Human Rights, ECLI:NL:RBDHA:2020:1878, The Hague. Accessed 5 Feb 2020
14. Valdivia, ; de la Cueva, J.: The paradox of efficiency: frictions between law and algorithms, VerfBlog (2022). https://verfassungsblog.de/roa-the-paradox-of-efficiency/, https://doi.org/10.17176/20220402-131142-0
15. Guadagnoli, G.: Open source, open data and public algorithms in France. The French public administration is opening up public data, algorithms and source codes. European Commission. https://joinup.ec.europa.eu/collection/open-source-observatory-osor/news/open-source-open-data-and-public-algorithms-france
16. Ponce Solé, J.: Some considerations on the relationship between humans and artificial intelligence: the "human reserve" and human supervision (human in/on the loop), draft submitted to Symposium Public Administration and the EU Proposal for a Regulation of Artificial Intelligence, Barcelona (2023)

17. Geuvers, H.: Proof assistants: history, ideas and future. Sādhanā **34**, 3–25 (2009)
18. de Almeida Borges, A., González Bedmar, M., Conejero Rodríguez, J., Hermo Reyes, E., Casals Buñuel, J., Joosten, J.J.: FV time: a formally verified CoQ library. arXiv preprint arXiv:2209.14227 (2022)
19. Müller, M., Joosten, J.J.: Model-checking in the foundations of algorithmic law and the case of regulation 561. arXiv preprint arXiv:2307.05658
20. Joosten, J.J., Montoya García, M., di Giustizia, L.N.: Interactions between artificial intelligence, law, logic, language and computation with some case studies in traffic regulations and health care. In: Ponce, J., Cerrillo, A. (eds.) The EU Artificial Intelligence Act and the Public Sector. Humans and AI systems in Public Administration in the light of the European Regulation on Artificial Intelligence of 2024, European Public Law Series/Bibliothèque de Droit Public Européen, Chapter 3, European Public Law Organizations (EPLO), Athens, In Press (2024)

A Web-Based Environment for the Specification and Generation of Smart Legal Contracts

Regan Meloche[1], Durga Sivakumar[1], Amal A. Anda[1], Sofana Alfuhaid[1,2], Daniel Amyot[1(✉)], Luigi Logrippo[1,3], and John Mylopoulos[1]

[1] University of Ottawa, Ottawa ON, K1N 6N5, Canada
{rmeloch2,dsiva066,aanda,salfu014,damyot,jmylopou}@uottawa.ca, luigi@uqo.ca
[2] King Abdulaziz University, Jeddah, Saudi Arabia
[3] Université du Québec en Outaouais, Gatineau QC, J8X 3X7, Canada
https://sites.google.com/uottawa.ca/csmlab/

Abstract. Monitoring the compliance of contract performance against legal obligations is important in order to detect violations, ideally, as soon as they occur. Such monitoring can nowadays be achieved through the use of smart contracts, which provide protection against tampering as well as some level of automation in handling violations. However, there exists a large gap between natural language contracts and smart contract implementations. This paper introduces a Web-based environment that partly fills that gap by supporting the user-assisted refinement of Symboleo specifications corresponding to legal contract templates, followed by the automated generation of monitoring smart contracts deployable on the Hyperledger Fabric platform. This environment, illustrated using a sample contract from the transactive energy domain, shows much potential in accelerating the development of smart contracts in a legal compliance context.

Keywords: Compliance Monitoring · Natural Language Processing · Smart Contract · Symboleo · Transactive Energy

1 Introduction

Legal contracts describe obligations and powers that apply to business transactions between parties playing roles such buyers and sellers, or service providers

Partially funded by NSERC's Strategic Partnership Grant *Middleware Framework and Programming Infrastructure for IoT Services*, by SSHRC's Partnership Grant *Autonomy Through Cyberjustice Technologies*, and by the ORF-RE project *CyPreSS: Software Techniques for the Engineering of Cyber-Physical Systems*.

© The Author(s), under exclusive license to Springer Nature Switzerland AG 2026
D. Restrepo Amariles and K. Satoh (Eds.): *Compliance for Artificial Intelligence Systems*, LNAI 14377, pp. 11–23, 2026.
https://doi.org/10.1007/978-3-032-12795-2_2

and consumers. Most often, they are redacted in Natural Language (NL). Violations of obligations may enable defined powers such as premature contract termination or penalties. They can also lead to costly conflict resolution mechanisms, including litigation in courts. Monitoring contract performance is important to detect such violations as early as possible, in order to favor potential alternative courses of actions and avoid litigation.

Nowadays, legal contracts can benefit from various automation strategies and technologies. For example, smart contracts are programs intended to partially automate legal contracts and monitor them for compliance with relevant terms and conditions. However, this paper uses a generic definition of smart contracts based on Szabo's [17], which is independent of the blockchain-based technologies commonly referenced in the past 15 years.

Contract templates capture standard clauses that enable their reuse (e.g., by selecting clauses), customization (e.g., through parameters), and refinement (e.g., by modifying clauses) for particular contexts. Such templates are particularly useful in situations where the type of business transaction targeted is well understood. One issue here is that refinement of a template may lead to an invalid contract (e.g., due to newly introduced inconsistencies) or to the unexpected dissatisfaction of desirable properties that the original template satisfied. Another issue is that the monitoring mechanisms supporting the original template may need to be updated to reflect such refinements.

One solution avenue for both problems is the use of an intermediate formalization of legal templates that supports both property verification and the generation of smart contracts that monitor legal contract executions [15]. For example, the SYMBOLEO language [14] can be used to specify contract templates in terms of parameterized obligations and powers, while enabling formal verification of properties [11] and the automated generation of monitoring smart contracts [13]. Although SYMBOLEO is supported by an Eclipse-based editor and automated code generators [14], the creation of formal specifications for contract templates and their refinements are currently done *manually*. Also, the Eclipse Integrated Development Environment (IDE) [4] is a desktop environment that requires many components to be installed locally, which is a major barrier to entry for many potential SYMBOLEO users.

In an effort to simplify and partially automate the generation and modification of SYMBOLEO specifications, this paper provides two main contributions:

- A Web-based tool (SYMBOLEONLP, https://bit.ly/SymboleoNLP) that handles part of the formalization of NL templates to SYMBOLEO specifications, with a focus on temporal and conditional refinements.
- A Web-based IDE (SYMBOLEOWEB, https://bit.ly/Symboleo_Web) that takes the generated SYMBOLEO, enables intelligent editing and validation, and converts it to executable smart contracts in JavaScript for the Hyperledger Fabric distributed ledger platform (https://www.hyperledger.org/projects/fabric). SYMBOLEOWEB simplifies the access to SYMBOLEO tools.

This composite Web-based environment is illustrated here using a *transactive energy* (TE) contract template example. TE markets already use smart contracts and are eager to support small-scale but automated contracts for trading energy between prosumers (i.e., consumers who also produce and sell energy).

The rest of this paper is as follows. Section 2 first presents related work in that area. Section 3 describes how SYMBOLEONLP helps generate SYMBOLEO specifications from refined NL templates, while Sect. 4 illustrates how SYMBOLEOWEB supports editing and code generation. An analysis of different refinements to a TE contract template in terms of their impact on the size of the SYMBOLEO specifications and JavaScript code generated is provided in Sect. 5. Finally, Sects. 6 and 7 present a discussion and our conclusions, respectively.

2 Related Work

There exist several formal specification languages for legal contracts [15] and for smart contracts [19]. Some support a certain degree of code generation from abstract specifications, while some support the formal verification of properties [7,19]. SYMBOLEO is unique since it enables both i) formal verification of desirable properties expressed in Linear Temporal Logic or in Computation Tree Logic [11], as well as ii) the automated generation of smart contracts (using the SYMBOLEO2SC [13] tool) deployable on the Hyperledger Fabric platform.

SYMBOLEO exploits a legal contract ontology with concepts such as obligation, power, party, role, asset, and event [14]. The language enables modelers to specify contracts by defining a domain model that extends this ontology, and then the legal obligations and powers that express legal clauses and terms.

SYMBOLEO has been used to specify different types of supply chain contracts that can benefit from automated monitoring of performance. This includes the transactive energy domain [10], where energy is the asset being sold from prosumers to buyers. TE contracts have also been coded manually by others as smart contracts running over different blockchain platforms [5,6].

One key issue is the generation of formal specifications from NL contracts. For the SYMBOLEO ontology, some preliminary work was done by Soavi et al. [16], but with limited automation. Meloche et al. [8,9] recently provided a higher level of automation in the generation of SYMBOLEO specifications, but only for certain categories of legal contracts *templates*. An unrefined template (T) is converted manually to SYMBOLEO (specification $S(T)$), and then manual refinements (C) of the original template, expressed using a controlled natural language (CNL) supported by a dynamic grammar, are automatically transformed into valid refinements of the specification ($S(C)$). We extend this work with a more complete translation and a web-based interface implemented in the SYMBOLEONLP tool.

Tateishi et al. [18] proposed a technique and a toolset for automatically generating a smart contract from a contract written in a CNL using a template-based approach. For a given contract domain, a contract template is manually created, which contains parameters that can be customized using the CNL. Given the template and the customizations, a formal model is automatically generated in a domain-specific language. The formal model can then be translated into smart contract code. The approach and goals are similar to SymboleoNLP, but a key difference is the scope of customized refinements. In this related work, the allowed customizations are specified individually for each parameter, meaning that the preparation can be quite tedious. SymboleoNLP's approach is to have a more general CNL that can be used with a large variety of template parameters. This important difference makes the initial set up process much easier.

Dwivedi et al. [3] developed a smart contract language (SCL) for decentralized autonomous organizations. SCL shares some ontological and technical similarities with Symboleo. For example, both approaches address the ability for certain norms to trigger the creation of other norms (e.g., the failure to complete an obligation can trigger the instantiation of a power to terminate the contract). A markup language to specify contracts (SCLML) is based on this ontology and can be converted to Solidity code for a smart contract implementation.

3 From Contract Templates to Symboleo

We can illustrate the process of formalizing refinements on a NL contract into Symboleo using a simple Transactive Energy (TE) contract, shown in Table 1.

Table 1. Simple TE contract with two refinement locations (P1, P2).

This agreement is entered into effect as of <date>, between <buyer> as Buyer and <prosumer> as Prosumer.
1. Prosumer shall dispatch <energy_qnt> kW of power to the Buyer **[P1]**.
2. The power needs to be dispatched to <location>.
3. The Buyer shall pay <amount> in CAD to the Prosumer **[P2]**.
4. In case of late payment, the Buyer shall pay a late fee equal to <percentage> of the
amount owed, and the Prosumer may suspend performance of all of its obligations under the agreement until payment of amounts owed has been received in full.
5. Any delay in the dispatching of the power, or any problem with the voltage (which must be between <min> V and <max> V), will entitle the Buyer to terminate the Contract.

From this contract, we will consider the first sentence, which specifies an obligation of the prosumer to dispatch an amount of power to the buyer. The obligation specifies that the power delivery must be made within a certain timeframe. The contract template allows for flexibility in choosing the start and end times of this timeframe. However, there may be cases where more flexibility is needed in the contract template. For example, we may want to specify that the power must be delivered *before* a certain date, *after* a certain date, or perhaps a more complex temporal specification (e.g., within 2 weeks of buyer paying the prosumer). SymboleoNLP is built to handle these more complex temporal refinements, as well as certain types of conditional refinements.

The process begins with a broadly-specified NL contract *T* and its corresponding SYMBOLEO specification *S(T)*, which, using our example sentence, are presented as follows:

- *T*: Prosumer shall dispatch <energy_qnt> kW of power to the buyer **[P1]**
- *S(T)*: `Obligation(Prosumer, Buyer, true, Happens(evt_dispatch_energy))`

Note that in practice, *T* and *S(T)* will correspond to full contracts. We simplify it here to correspond to only one sentence for illustrative purposes. The full SYMBOLEO contract will also include more detailed definitions of the Prosumer and Buyer roles, as well as of `evt_dispatch_energy`, which specifies the event that must happen to fulfill the obligation. We omit details for conciseness.

The artifacts *T* and *S(T)* are fed to the SYMBOLEONLP tool, and the contract author can make temporal and conditional refinements on the parameter [P1] in *T*. The refinements that the contract author is allowed to specify come from a carefully-constructed CNL that is based on a dataset of legal contract refinements [8,9]. These refinements often come in the form of a linguistic *adjunct*, a component of a sentence that adds information, but when removed from the sentence, does not alter the basic sentence structure. Adjuncts often add information about time, space, or method, and they can take various grammatical forms, including prepositional phrases and adverbs. Some examples of adjuncts that may be allowed in the CNL for this refinement include: i) *between [START_DATE] and [END_DATE]*; ii) *before March 31, 2023*; and iii) *within 2 weeks of the buyer paying the prosumer*. Note how these two prepositional phrases add extra information to the sentence, but are *not* required for the sentence to be complete; They simply restrict the meaning, which is the function of adjuncts.

The first adjunct example is often found in a typical TE contract, so we will use this as an example. Traditional contract template programs may simply allow a user to fill in the two dates, but SYMBOLEONLP allows a contract author a higher degree of customizability in how the contract is refined, by accommodating these more complex grammatical structures. Once the user enters and submits the refinement (see typical sequence in Figs. 1, 2 and 3), SYMBOLEONLP will automatically formalize the refined NL contract into the corresponding SYMBOLEO specification. This specification is now ready to be used in the SYMBOLEOWEB project, as we illustrate in Sect. 4.

4 SYMBOLEO Editing and SC Code Generation

This section discusses SYMBOLEOWEB, our new web-based environment to help edit SYMBOLEO specifications and generate smart contracts from them. Figures 4 and 5 illustrate this tool. The code and a deployed version are available online[1].

SYMBOLEOWEB primarily uses Microsoft's Monaco editor[2], which has become a cornerstone of various applications, most notably serving as the code

[1] https://bit.ly/Symboleo_Web.
[2] https://microsoft.github.io/monaco-editor/.

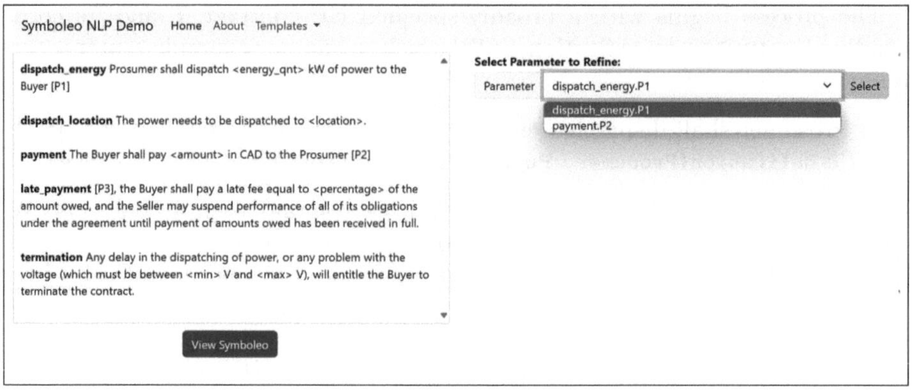

Fig. 1. The user selects the parameter to refine.

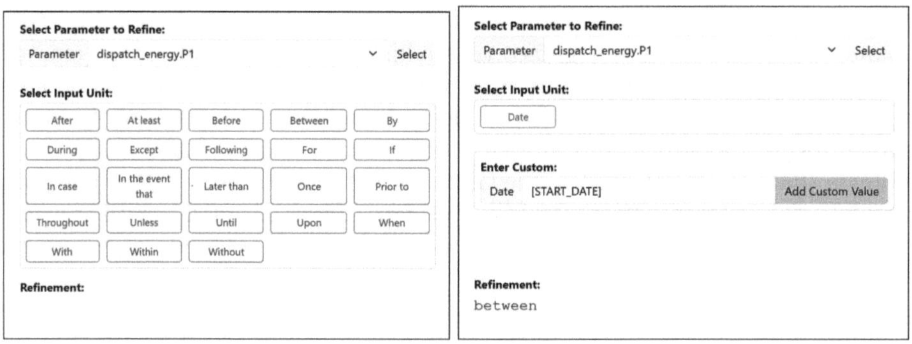

Fig. 2. Left: The user enters the refinement according to the text values allowed by the CNL. In some cases, the user is given a set of fixed text values to choose from. Right: In other cases, the CNL allows the user to enter certain values, such as the date.

editor for Visual Studio Code (VSCode). The editor supports a myriad of programming languages, boasts features such as syntax highlighting, autocompletion, and error diagnostics, and is renowned for its responsive user interface. This is combined with LSP4J[3], a Java implementation of the *Language Server Protocol* (LSP), to be used by language servers built using Java. The LSP defines the communication protocol used between an editor/IDE and a language server. By complying with LSP, the server can be used by any client (VSCode desktop application, Web IDE, etc.). The *WebSocket Secure* (WSS) protocol[4] is also used to facilitate communication between the client and the language server.

Figure 4 illustrates a TE SYMBOLEO specification as seen in SYMBOLEOWEB. In this example, the contract specification contains an error in line 18, which is correctly highlighted as such. Furthermore, hovering over an error gives useful

[3] https://github.com/eclipse-lsp4j/lsp4j.
[4] https://websockets.spec.whatwg.org/.

```
Contract TransactiveEnergy (
  prosumer_id: String,
  buyer_id: String,
  amount_kw: Number,
  amount: Number,
  currency: Currency,
  percentage: Number,
  min_voltage: Number,
  max_voltage: Number,
  start_date: Date,
  end_date: Date,
)
Declarations
  prosumer: Prosumer;
  buyer: Buyer;
  energy: Energy with amount_kw := <energy_qnt>;
  evt_dispatch: DispatchEnergy with energy := energy, dispatcher := prosumer, recipient := buyer;
  evt_pay: Pay with amount := <amount>, currency := Currency(CAD), from := buyer, to := prosumer;
  evt_pay_interest: PayInterest with amount := "(1 + <percentage> / 100) * <amount>", currency := Currency(CAD), from := buyer, to
:= prosumer;

Obligations
  ob_dispatch: O(prosumer, buyer, true, HappensWithin(evt_dispatch, Interval(start_date, end_date)));
  ob_payment: O(buyer, prosumer, true, Happens(evt_pay));
  ob_pay_interest: O(buyer, prosumer, true, Happens(evt_pay_interest));
```

Fig. 3. The SYMBOLEO code is now updated with the required changes (to the domain model and event monitoring predicate) introduced by the refinement.

insights into how the error might be resolved. For example, in line 6, the editor suggests how to properly auto-complete a parameter type that starts with `B` (user-defined types are also suggested). The implementation of the validation and auto-completion rules defined by Rasti [12] contributes to improving the productivity of the user manually editing SYMBOLEO specifications.

Finally, as shown in Fig. 5, once the server recognizes an error-free SYMBOLEO specification, it automatically invokes SYMBOLEO2SC [13] to generate the corresponding smart contract code in JavaScript, including the different assets, roles, obligations, events, etc. The user can view (and even edit, although this is not recommended) the generated files directly in SYMBOLEOWEB or (more likely) download them for direct deployment over the Hyperledger Fabric platform.

While SYMBOLEOWEB can be used to build a SYMBOLEO contract from scratch, it can be especially useful when used in concert with SYMBOLEONLP, as it exemplifies the flow from NL refinement to SYMBOLEO specification, and then to executable code. SYMBOLEONLP relies on various natural language processing and machine learning techniques, some of which are probabilistic [9], and can lead to slight errors in the SYMBOLEO generation. SYMBOLEOWEB provides easy and intuitive means for a human user to correct these mistakes.

5 Analysis

We conducted an empirical analysis to assess the impact of NL template refinements on the resulting SYMBOLEO specifications and smart contracts in JavaScript (JS). This also indirectly helps assess potential time and effort saved. We applied five distinct refinements, and four combinations thereof, to an initial NL contract template with two refinement locations ([P1] and [P2] in Table 1):

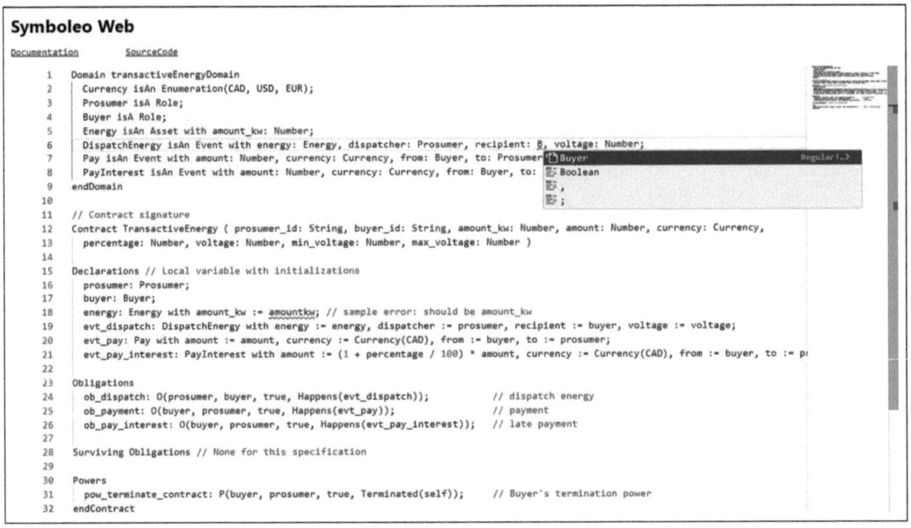

Fig. 4. Online SymboleoWeb editor, with syntax highlight, error reporting, and code completion for Symboleo specifications.

1. R1 (P_1) = between [START_DATE] and [END_DATE]
2. R2 (P_2) = before March 31, 2024
3. R3 (P_2) = within 2 weeks of Prosumer dispatching energy
4. R4 (P_1) = before March 31, 2024
5. R5 (P_1) = within 2 weeks of Buyer paying Prosumer.
6. R1R2 (P_1, P_2): *Refinements R1 and R2*
7. R1R3 (P_1, P_2): *Refinements R1 and R3*
8. R4R2 (P_1, P_2): *Refinements R4 and R2*
9. R4R3 (P_1, P_2): *Refinements R4 and R3*

First, an initial Symboleo specification of the TE contract was created from a broadly specified NL contract and its corresponding specification (Sect. 3). SymboleoNLP was then used to generate our 9 refinements of the contract, each as a Symboleo file. These 9 specifications, together with the initial one, were fed to SymboleoWeb to generate the corresponding 10 smart contracts. Table 2 shows the results of our empirical analysis, where we measure the lines of code (LOC) that were added, modified, and deleted by several refinements to the initial Symboleo contract and corresponding JS smart contract. The LOC metric is often used as a proxy measure of development time and effort.

As shown in Table 2, the Symboleo specifications of the contract and its refinements contain ~41 LOC, while on average the corresponding smart contracts contain ~618 LOC, resulting in an average LOC expansion ratio of about 1:15 (excluding the ~3,000 LOC of JS code composing the Symboleo library, invoked by the generated code). The percentage of changed JS LOC varies from 2.1% to 8.1%, with the highest amount of changes corresponding to the more

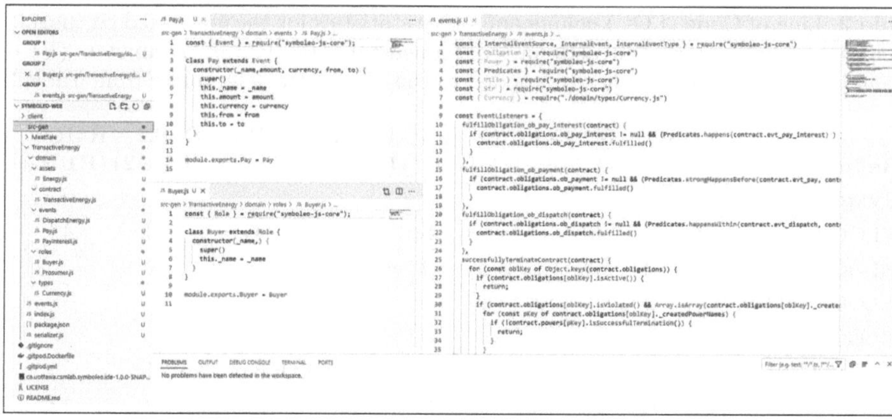

Fig. 5. SymboleoWeb editor showing the generated smart contract code (in JavaScript) for the initial Symboleo specification (Fig. 4), with example files for an event, a role, and the event management.

complex refinements (based on R3 and R5). These findings collectively provide insights into the nature of refinements in the context of Symboleo contracts. As these changes also impact multiple files, doing this manually would be both a time-consuming and error-prone maintenance activity. The sustained consistency in the ratios between specification sizes and generated code sizes also suggests relatively predictable time and effort savings over manual approaches. Finally, such savings grow with the number and complexity of NL refinements applied.

6 Discussion

Methods and tools for helping in the smart contract creation, validation, and performance-monitoring have an immediate application to platforms where formalized contract templates with fixed variations are already in use, such as the mentioned transactive energy domain. In this area, the need is quite real, to support the practice of rapidly switching between power sources according to unpredictable swings in supply and demand. Performance could be automatic, including for example the payment of penalties from funds set aside for this purpose. Other concrete examples of applicable fields include:

- **Online E-commerce platforms:** These platforms are now limited to fixed and extremely simple contractual formats, with very few choices. One can envisage marketplaces where one of the parties, usually the seller, would offer a wider range of choices, to be selected by the other party. For example, different 'powers' can be offered to the other party to cover different circumstances such as the possibility of delivering certain products rather than others, or proposing different delivery options for different payments. The contract performance monitor would guide the parties through the steps necessary to realize the selected scenario.

Table 2. Line of Code (LOC) counts and other statistics for the generated SYMBOLEO specifications and smart contracts for five refinements (R1–R5) of parameters (P1 or P2) and four combinations thereof applied to the TE contract template from Table 1.

Refinements:	**Init**	**R1 (P1)**	**R2 (P2**	**R3 (P2)**	**R4 (P1)**	**R5 (P1)**	**R1R2 (P1,P2)**	**R1R3 (P1,P2)**	**R4R2 (P1,P2)**	**R4R3 (P1,P2)**
SYMBOLEO										
#LOC	40	40	40	41	40	42	40	41	40	41
#LOC added		0	0	1	0	2	0	1	0	1
#LOC modified		2	2	3	2	1	3	4	3	6
#LOC deleted		0	0	0	0	0	0	0	0	0
Smart Contract (SC), in JavaScript (JS), for Hyperledger Fabric										
No. of file	12	12	12	12	12	13	12	12	12	12
#LOC SC	606	608	607	630	607	647	609	632	608	631
#LOC added		2	3	32	3	41	9	34	8	33
#LOC modified		11	12	5	11	4	6	9	6	9
#LOC deleted		0	2	8	2	0	6	8	6	8
%LOC changed		2.1%	2.5%	7.1%	2.6%	7.0%	3.4%	8.1%	3.3%	7.9%
Ratio SC/Sym	15.2	14.5	14.8	15.4	14.5	15.8	14.2	14.7	14.5	15.0

- **Supply chain monitoring:** Throughout the supply chain, perishable food must adhere to specific standards, for purposes of health and traceability. Certain contracts may require that the food being transported stay within a specific temperature range, or that the food be delivered under specific conditions and/or within a specific time frame. Sensors and tracking devices could be configured to communicate with the smart contract, notifying it of events that are related to the fulfillment or violation of certain obligations.

Several approaches that formalize norms and enable their validation, including eFLINT [1,2] (which also offers a Web-based interface), only provide partial solutions to the above scenarios, whereas our Web-based environment for SYMBOLEO goes further, with deployable monitoring smart contracts.

At this point, SYMBOLEONLP supports the formalization of a variety of temporal and conditional refinements, but future work may involve expanding the functionality to formalize more complex semantics. In most cases, the SYMBOLEO code generated by SYMBOLEONLP requires a small amount of manual revision and clean up, primarily minor formatting issues with the contract parameters. While the controlled NL used in SYMBOLEONLP allows for the specification of simple events, there are some important limitations. The events that can be represented are restricted to simple events in an active form. Future work involves empirically deriving a more sophisticated event specification based on real contract data, which may include subordinate clauses, negations, and conjunctions. The refinements used in the analysis were all temporal in nature, but we can also imagine the parameters being filled with other types of adjuncts, such as *condi-*

tionals. For example, we may want to specify that the energy must be delivered to the buyer *if the market price for energy exceeds a predetermined threshold set by the buyer*. While these types of operations are supported by SYMBOLEONLP, they are limited by the simplified specification of events.

It may also be useful, particularly in the transactive energy domain, to specify state-based conditionals in the contract. For example, if the voltage of the dispatched energy is not within certain bounds, then there might be a financial penalty for the prosumer. While SYMBOLEONLP includes conditional-based refinements, these are restricted to conditionals that include events. Future work may involve allowing for NL refinements that reflect *state-based* conditions.

SYMBOLEONLP currently operates with a CNL, since this allows for more predictable mappings to the formal specification. We may want to relax the refinements to allow for more freeform input, which would in turn allow for more expressiveness for the contract author. The trade-off for that expressiveness would be a reduction in its ability to properly formalize the refinement. However, future work may involve exploring the application of Large Language Models (LLMs) to this problem, which could potentially mitigate this reduction.

7 Conclusion

Legal contracts play a crucial role in business transactions between parties, and violating their obligations can lead to serious consequences. Smart contracts have been introduced to effectively monitor the performance providing early alerts for potential violations in contract performance. This paper presents practical and accessible solutions for formalizing contract templates and addressing challenges associated with template refinement and monitoring mechanisms.

Our practical approach involves two complementary Web-based tools: SYMBOLEONLP utilizes temporal and conditional refinements to convert NL templates into SYMBOLEO specifications. Subsequently, these specifications are processed by the second tool, SYMBOLEOWEB, which validates and transforms them into smart contracts using SYMBOLEO2SC. We evaluated the tools with a transactive energy contract example and an empirical analysis involving multiple refinements. Although our results are currently limited to one template, the key finding indicates a stable refinement process, as evidenced by a consistent ratio between specifications and generated code, and percentages of changes that grow with the number and complexity of NL refinements, which suggest corresponding time and effort savings as our approach is automated.

In addition to the points raised in the previous section, future work involves a tighter integration of the two tools and of the SYMBOLEOPC property checker [11], additional performance experiments and improvements, further extensions of the smart contract code generator to better support security and other non-functional aspects, and formal usability studies involving real users.

References

1. van Binsbergen, L.T.: Reflections on the design and application of eFLINT. In: Programming Languages and the Law (ProLaLa) (2022). http://ltvanbinsbergen.nl/files/abstracts/prolala2022.pdf
2. van Binsbergen, L.T., Liu, L.C., van Doesburg, R., van Engers, T.: EFLINT: a domain-specific language for executable norm specifications. In: GPCE 2020, pp. 124–136. ACM (2020). https://doi.org/10.1145/3425898.3426958
3. Dwivedi, V., et al.: A formal specification smart-contract language for legally binding decentralized autonomous organizations. IEEE Access **9**, 76069–76082 (2021). https://doi.org/10.1109/ACCESS.2021.3081926
4. Eclipse Foundation: Eclipse ide (2023). https://eclipseide.org/
5. Khan, K., Ahmed, T., Cali, U., Arboleya, P., Grybniak, S., El-Sayed, I.: A definitive technology stack for development of smart contracts for energy applications. In: 2023 IEEE Power & Energy Society General Meeting (PESGM), pp. 1–5 (2023). https://doi.org/10.1109/PESGM52003.2023.10253128
6. Kirli, D., et al.: Smart contracts in energy systems: a systematic review of fundamental approaches and implementations. Renew. Sustain. Energy Rev. **158**, 112013 (2022). https://doi.org/10.1016/j.rser.2021.112013
7. Krichen, M., Lahami, M., Al-Haija, Q.A.: Formal methods for the verification of smart contracts: a review. In: 2022 15th International Conference on Security of Information and Networks (SIN), pp. 01–08 (2022). https://doi.org/10.1109/SIN56466.2022.9970534
8. Meloche, R.: Formalizing contract refinements using a controlled natural language, Master's thesis, University of Ottawa, Canada (2023). https://doi.org/10.20381/ruor-29889
9. Meloche, R., Amyot, D., Mylopoulos, J.: Towards legal contract formalization with controlled natural language templates. In: 2023 IEEE 31st International Requirements Engineering Conference (RE). pp. 317–322 (2023). https://doi.org/10.1109/RE57278.2023.00042
10. Parvizimosaed, A., Bashari, M., Kian, A.R., Amyot, D., Mylopoulos, J.: Compliance checking for transactive energy contracts using smart contracts. In: 2020 IEEE PES Transactive Energy Systems Conference (TESC), pp. 1–5 (2020). https://doi.org/10.1109/TESC50295.2020.9656942
11. Parvizimosaed, A., Roveri, M., Rasti, A., Amyot, D., Logrippo, L., Mylopoulos, J.: Model-checking legal contracts with SymboleoPC. In: Proceedings of the 25th International Conference on Model Driven Engineering Languages and Systems, pp. 278–288. MODELS '22, ACM (2022). https://doi.org/10.1145/3550355.3552449
12. Rasti, A.: From Symboleo to smart contracts - a code generator, Master's thesis, University of Ottawa, Canada (2023). https://doi.org/10.20381/ruor-28394
13. Rasti, A., et al.: Automated generation of smart contract code from legal contract specifications with Symboleo2SC. Softw. Syst. Model. (2024). https://doi.org/10.1007/s10270-024-01187-9
14. Sharifi, S., Parvizimosaed, A., Amyot, D., Logrippo, L., Mylopoulos, J.: Symboleo: towards a specification language for legal contracts. In: 2020 IEEE 28th International Requirements Engineering Conference (RE), pp. 364–369 (2020). https://doi.org/10.1109/RE48521.2020.00049
15. Soavi, M., Zeni, N., Mylopoulos, J., Mich, L.: From legal contracts to formal specifications: a systematic literature review. SN Comput. Sci. **3**(5), 345 (2022). https://doi.org/10.1007/s42979-022-01228-4

16. Soavi, M., Zeni, N., Mylopoulos, J., Mich, L.: Semantic annotation of legal contracts with Contrattoa. Informatics **9**(4) (2022). https://doi.org/10.3390/informatics9040072
17. Szabo, N.: Formalizing and securing relationships on public networks. In: First Monday (1997). https://doi.org/10.5210/fm.v2i9.548
18. Tateishi, T., Yoshihama, S., Sato, N., Saito, S.: Automatic smart contract generation using controlled natural language and template. IBM J. Res. Dev. **63**(2/3), 6:1–6:12 (2019). https://doi.org/10.1147/JRD.2019.2900643
19. Tolmach, P., Li, Y., Lin, S.W., Liu, Y., Li, Z.: A survey of smart contract formal specification and verification. ACM Comput. Surv. **54**(7) (2022). https://doi.org/10.1145/3464421

GDPR120Q: An Annotated Q&A Corpus for Privacy Compliance

Raphaël Gyory[1(✉)], Grégory Lewkowicz[1], David Restrepo Amariles[2], Sébastien Meeùs[1], Simone Casalena[1], and Hugues Bersini[1]

[1] Université Libre de Bruxelles, Brussels, Belgium
{raphael.gyory,gregory.lewkowicz,sebastien.meeus,simone.casalena, hugues.bersini}@ulb.be
[2] HEC Paris, Paris, France
restrepo-amariles@hec.fr

Abstract. Ensuring compliance with data privacy regulations and policies poses a challenge for organizations. Natural Legal Language Processing (NLLP) using deep learning presents a promising avenue for addressing this challenge. A critical hindrance to fully harnessing the potential of machine learning techniques in privacy compliance is the limited availability of extensive, domain-specific labeled datasets. In response to this critical gap, this paper introduces GDPR120Q, a new specialized, expert-annotated question-answering dataset, which we used to test for formal compliance of privacy documents with the European Union General Data Protection Regulation (GDPR). GDPR120Q consists of 39,834 annotations, 120 recent privacy policies, 108 possible labels and is, to date, the only open-source large-scale dataset dealing with privacy issues under European law. We leverage this dataset to identify text spans in privacy policies that require attention from individuals and data processors for compliance purposes. We test the dataset with baseline transformer models as well as GPT3, which return promising results but leave substantial room for improvement. As one of the only large, specialized NLP annotated by experts, GDPR120Q can contribute to the development of innovative approaches to privacy compliance and serves as a benchmark for the NLLP community.

Keywords: Annotated dataset · Benchmark · GDPR · Privacy compliance · Legal NLP

1 Introduction

According to Villata et al. [79], the recent and significant developments in Natural Legal Language Processing (NLLP) are driven by three interrelated factors: the development of new technologies such as large pre-trained Transformers [23], the interest for legal applications in a growing number of domains, and finally, the availability of legal corpora. Specialized legal corpora, particularly expert annotated datasets that provide the ground truth for training and evaluating

© The Author(s), under exclusive license to Springer Nature Switzerland AG 2026
D. Restrepo Amariles and K. Satoh (Eds.): *Compliance for Artificial Intelligence Systems*, LNAI 14377, pp. 24–48, 2026.
https://doi.org/10.1007/978-3-032-12795-2_3

algorithms, are crucial because they calibrate the extent to which language models can be developed for or adapted to the highly specialized field of law [34]. However, the development of domain-specific datasets, annotated by experts, is costly. This approach is primarily justifiable in the highly valuable legal domains, either in terms of scale or in relation to tasks with significant legal or financial added value. Privacy compliance is one of these domains, especially in the European Union, for three reasons.

Firstly, privacy compliance is expensive for organizations operating in the European Union, especially since the introduction of the GDPR in 2018 [6, 77]. The GDPR sets high data protection and privacy compliance standards [85] and penalties for breaching its obligations can go up to №20 million or 4% of the organization's global annual turnover. The importance of complying with the GDPR is not limited to the financial implications for data processors. Compliance also ensures individual's privacy is protected and helps build trust between organizations and consumers [4,74,80].

In 2018, when GPDR entered into force, the average budget spent by firms to comply with GDPR was $13.2 million, rising to $13.6 million in 2019 [38]. Compliance costs vary depending on factors like company size, industry, and geography. For example, the FTSE 100 stock index companies in 2018 had estimated compliance costs ranging from $84 million for banks to $6 million for industrial goods and services firms [20,40]. A significant portion of these costs is attributed to hiring privacy compliance personnel (20–50% of the costs), and outside consultants and lawyers (19–24%) to work on data inventory tasks as well as the handling of data subject requests, which are partially automatable tasks [20]. For firms exposed to the regulation, it was said that it leads to an 8% decline in profits and a 2% reduction in sales [21]. The increase of GDPR compliance costs from year to year is a trend that has been confirmed in the literature [25].

Secondly, from the consumer's perspective, privacy policies are almost incomprehensible because they are time-consuming, full of jargon and lead to an information overload [52,54,59,68]. Cranor [54] estimated already in 2008 that an individual would need an average of 201 h a year to read all the privacy policies they encounter. Obar [59] highlights that the majority of users simply skip the privacy policies and terms of service. In this context, any tools for legal simplification at scale can be a valuable contribution to the effectiveness of data subject rights.

Finally, personal data protection is closely linked to the development of other compliance technologies, as it represents a prerequisite for their implementation [39,64]. Developers of such technologies must, for example, guarantee the right to a rectification of the data provided to the system (GDPR art. 16), the right to objection to the creation of profiles that are not specifically allowed (GDPR art. 19) and the right to be forgotten (GDPR art. 21). Therefore, a GDPR-compliant data pipeline is of tremendous importance and a "special focus must be given to the origin of the analyzed data" used by technological companies in their decision-making processes [64].

Considering the various potential benefits of NLLP for privacy compliance, we introduce in this paper GDPR120Q, an annotated dataset of question-answers pairs that aims to contribute to Document to Regulation Compliance within the framework of the European General Data Protection Regulation (GDPR).

The purpose of this paper is to introduce the GDPR120Q dataset and evaluate the performance of baseline models that have been trained on it and use our annotations. Section 2 introduces the context in which GDPR120Q was developed and the needs it addresses. Section 3 describes the related research and shows the singularity of GDPR120Q as the only open-source large-scale dataset dealing with privacy issues under European law. In Sect. 4, we describe the labelling process of the GDPR120Q dataset. In Sect. 5, we examine the outcomes of various tests conducted to benchmark GDPR120Q to support the assertion that expert-annotated, domain-specific datasets are essential for developing innovative solutions in legal compliance. The final section presents our conclusions as well as opportunities for future research.

2 A Benchmark for Document to Regulation Compliance in the Context of GDPR

The GDPR is a comprehensive regulation that grants data protection rights to data subjects, prescribes how data processors must process personal data, and establishes procedures to verify compliance with the regulation's provisions. Transparency obligations are contained in Articles 13 and 14 to ensure data processing is carried out according to information that has been made explicit to the data subject. The transparency obligations are fulfilled in practice through privacy policies. Their function is to comply with the transparency obligations by providing information to users about the conditions established by state laws and regulations to process their data. For instance, articles 13 and 14 of the GDPR, establish, among others, that data subjects have to be informed in a clear manner about their rights, the legal basis for processing personal data, and the purposes of such processing.

As economic assets [46,69], personal data are susceptible to inter-organizational transfers. The potentially high complexity of these transfers gave rise to the concept of data supply chain [8,30], which emphasizes that data can flow through several actors âĂŞ (sub-)processors âĂŞ besides the original holder and controller. Ensuring compliance throughout the data supply chain requires significant investments for organizations in terms of processes, people, and technology, notably because organizations often lack a robust, comprehensive approach and carry out most privacy compliance tasks manually [20,48].

Restrepo Amariles et al. [8] provide a roadmap and defined set of tasks to leverage machine learning for compliance checking in the context of GDPR. One of the key preliminary tasks they identify is to conceptualize compliance in the data supply chain and identify the relevant methods [8]. El Hamdani et al. [30] and Meeùs [55] subsequently introduced a conceptual framework of compliance in the data supply chain under the GDPR. This approach is structured around the following tasks:

1. Document to Regulation (Formal and Substantial) Compliance, where the compliance of a document is assessed against a regulation (here, the GDPR), both in form and in substance.
2. Document Chain Compliance, where the documents are assessed against the main contractual standards or against documents with a higher hierarchy in the chain (for example, when entering into a licensing agreement with a third-party provider, the contract must be reviewed to ensure that it aligns with the organization's privacy policy).
3. Operational compliance, which checks that the practice described in one or more documents is actually carried out by the relevant stakeholder (i.e., data is erased at the end of the data retention period).

A task in Document to Regulation Formal Compliance is related to the categories of information data controllers must provide to data subjects, such as the legal basis, purposes of the processing or contact details. The categories are not determined at the sole discretion of the data controller, but are listed in Articles 13 and 14 of the GDPR, and are therefore mandatory information [55].

Consider the example of a web company that collects personal data and transfers it to a co-contractor to produce analytics. According to the GDPR, privacy policies must provide data subjects information about the retention period (Art. 13.2(a), e.g., two years). In this case, the purpose of Document to Regulation Formal Compliance is to provide a first-level review by identifying the presence or absence of information about data retention in the original policy. In turn, Document Chain Compliance refers to the conformity of the terms of the contract agreed between the web company and the co-contractor, with the terms of privacy policy agreed between the data subject and the web-company. The compliance chain must move along the data supply chain and therefore includes all the sub-contractors involved, including the sub-contractors of sub-contractors. In this context, the task related to Document Chain Compliance consists in verifying if the data retention periods agreed in the contracts downstream in the data supply chain correspond to the data retention period agreed in the privacy policy. Finally, Operational Compliance will check if the data has been effectively deleted from the servers of data processors and controllers when the retention period ends.

GDPR120Q addresses the first stage of privacy compliance, Document to Regulation Formal Compliance, which forms the foundation for the compliance review in the rest of the data supply chain. This task is hardly achievable today, either because the existing datasets are not GDPR aware, or because they lack granularity as indicated in Sect. 3. The dataset was developed to provide a new benchmark to help individuals and legal professionals assess the quality of the tools and methods used to review privacy policies.

3 Related Work

The annotation of a corpus for the purpose of privacy policy review is related to the areas of privacy compliance and contract review. We analyze the existing corpora and evaluate two dimensions: the granularity of the annotations and the GDPR awareness of the task.

3.1 Privacy Compliance

Granularity refers to the precision of the annotations, which can be performed at the span-level, the sentence or paragraph-level, or can categorize policies as a whole. Span-level annotations are more accurate and detailed and have been preferred for the seminal works in the field of both privacy compliance [83] and contract review [34]. A span-based approach reduces the "burden of searching the target information from a lengthy text segment" [3] and is also preferred in other fields, such as precision medicine [44, 58].

GDPR awareness refers to the extent to which the conceptual model used for the annotation of the data takes into account the concepts, rights and obligations included in the GDPR. As shown in Table 1, GDPR120Q is, to our knowledge, the only open-sourced, large-scale GDPR-aware effort to annotate privacy policies at the span level. A proprietary effort was recently carried out by the Centre for Security, Reliability and Trust of the University of Luxembourg [7, 16], which annotated fund management privacy policies at the span level as part of their research on the building of an NLP pipeline for AI-assisted completeness checking. Table 1 does not include this dataset because it has not been made available to the public.

The seminal work in the field of privacy compliance is OPP-115 [83], produced within the framework of the Usable Privacy Policy Project[1]. OPP-115 is a corpus of 115 privacy policies with 23.000 manual annotations. Annotations target text tokens and implement ten main label categories spanning 138 possible sublabels. This research, however, predates the GDPR. Follow-up research has been carried out to map the GDPR to this dataset. For example, Qamar and all offer paragraph-level annotations of both the OPP-115 privacy policies and the GDPR and created a correlation scheme to map the contents of a privacy policy to the appropriate segments of law it must conform to [62].

The other existing datasets are characterized either by their smaller granularity or by their lack of consideration of the GDPR. GDPR-aware corpora have been published by Tesfay [75], Bannihatti Kumar [11] and Ahmad [2]. Tesfay et al. provide 443 passages of 45 policies categorizing sentences into 11 categories. Bannihatti Kumar et al. provide annotations to identify opt-out hyperlinks, following the GDPR predating work of Sathyendra et al. [66]. Ahmad et al. refer to the GDPR but only in at the data post-processing step, where they asked experts to ensure their policies refer to four specific practices targeted by the GDPR (data collection/usage, data sharing/disclosure, data storage/retention, data security/protection). GDPR unaware corpora include the APP-350 Corpus [91] which contains 350 paragraph-level annotated Android app privacy policies, the Privacy Q&A Corpus [65] which contain 35 sentence-level annotated privacy policies, and PolicyQA [3] which extends OPP-115, adding 25,000 questions and

[1] https://usableprivacy.org/.

Table 1. The available privacy datasets sorted by year of publication. For each policy, we indicate whether it is GDPR compliant, annotated at the span level and provide its task type.

Corpus	GDPR	Span-level	Task type
OPP-115 [83]		•	Multi-label token classification
Opt-out dataset [66]			Binary sentence classification
Polisis [31]		•	Unannotated policies
Tesfay [75]	•		Multi-label sentence classification
Shvartzshnaider et al. [71]		•	Multi-class token classification
APP-350 Corpus [91]			Multi-label paragraph classification
PrivacyQA [65]			Binary sentence classification
Opt-out hyperlink dataset [11]	•		Binary token classification
PolicyQA [3]		•	Q&A
PolicyIE [2]	-	•	Multi-class token classification
PI-Extract [15]		•	Multi-label tokens classification
100K+ web privacy [57]			Multi-class document classification
GDPR correlation dataset [62]	•		Multi-label paragraph classification
PrivaSeer [73]	•		Unannotated policies
Princeton Leuven dataset [9]	•		Unannotated policies
GDPR120Q	•	•	Q&A

answers to the dataset. PI-Extract categorizes tokens in four categories determining whether data is collected and shared [15].

Larger datasets have been published but they provide a much lower granularity from the perspective of annotations. Zaeem & al. [57] released a corpus classifying 100K+ web privacy policies into 15 categories, such as "science", "arts" or "health". Wagner [81] collected a large-scale longitudinal corpus of privacy policies from 1996 to 2021 and uses NLP to describe the evolution of the data practices they contain. The Princeton Leuven dataset [9] is also a large-scale corpus providing statistical insights about the evolution of 130K policies over 20 years. Polisis [31] and TDLR [5] are large GDPR-unaware auto-annotated corpus of policies published along with frameworks for auto-annotation. The PrivaSeer corpus [73] contains 1,005,380 English language website privacy policies collected from the web and was used by its authors to perform unsupervised topic modeling and pretrain PrivBERT, a BERT based language model for privacy, a path already followed by Chalkidis et al. [19] for pretraining the LEGAL-BERT model.

Other privacy related research includes the work of Audich et al. [10], who study alternatives to expert annotations, such as crowdsourcing and algorithms for keyword extraction. Shvartzshnaider et al. [71] study the information flows in privacy policies and rely on 48 excerpts of privacy policies from 17 companies with 141 crowdworkers for testing information exchange. The authors compare the changes introduced post GDPR but do not focus on GDPR compliance.

3.2 Contract Review

The most ambitious research in the field of contract review is CUAD [34], a corpus of 13,000+ labels in 510 commercial legal contracts.

Other contract review datasets focus on narrow tasks. LEDGAR [78] and the dataset introduced by Chalkidis et al. [18] contain contracts annotated for named entity recognition. LEDGAR was constructed semi-automatically and contains 12.000 annotations in 60.000 contracts scraped from the public domain (SEC filings). Chalkidis et al.'s dataset contains 3000+ contracts and ten categories. ContractNLI [43] and the Lease Contract Review dataset [45] perform contract review at the text span level. ContractNLI is a crowd-worker-annotated dataset containing 7191 Natural Language Inference questions about spans of non-disclosure agreements. The Lease Contract Review dataset contains 179 lease contracts and approximately 3000 annotations categorizing text spans either as containing an entity or a red flag (2 categories). CLAUDETTE [49] is an expert-annotated dataset for identifying unfair clauses in terms of services. The dataset contains 50 documents with 1,032 annotations performed at the clause level, relating to eight categories. MAUD [82] provides multiple-choice questions in the field of merger and acquisition on a per clause basis.

4 Description of GDPR120Q

GDPR120Q was developed in a year-long interdisciplinary research effort involving legal experts, machine learning researchers and dozens of law students, under the initiative and coordination of the Smart Law Hub. The GDPR120Q dataset is available on the website of the Smart Law Hub[2].

4.1 Data

GDPR120Q contains 120 privacy policies and 39,834 annotations. The policies are from 8 industries: telecommunication (14 policies), retail (14 policies), entertainment (14 policies), social networks (14 policies), video games (16 policies), health (11 policies), finance (9 policies) and a broadly defined "service" category (28 policies).

We show the distribution of the policies' lengths in terms of tokens in Fig. 1. The policies vary substantially in length, ranging from 1000 to nearly 25000 tokens. We computed the number of tokens using the Bert tokenizer from the HuggingFace Transformers library [84]. The average policy length is 6492 tokens.

The policies come from applications available on the Google App Store. We retrieved their content from the vendors' site in April 2022.

[2] http://gdpr120.smartlawhub.eu/.

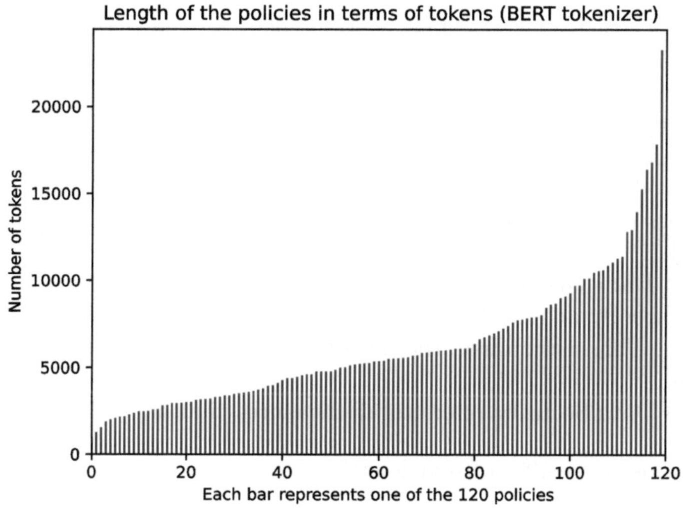

Fig. 1. A histogram showing the length of the GDPR120Q policies.

4.2 Labels

Our research uses the conceptual model designed by Torre et al. [76], but differs from it in several respects. First, we extended the scope of Torre's conceptual model with the addition of multiple selected resources: the W3C vocabulary to increase the granularity of the processing purposes [60], the OPP-115 categories of data [83], and the BPR4GDPR project ontology [88], for a total of 108 possible labels. These labels belong to 14 main categories:

1. Controller. This section includes references to the controller's identity and contact information.
2. Controller Representative. This section includes references to the controller representative's identity and contact information.
3. Data protection officer (DPO). This section includes references to the DPO's identity and contact information.
4. Personal data category. This section lists different categories of personal data, such as demographic, financial, or cookie information.
5. Processing Purpose. This section categorizes the purposes for processing data, such as commercial interests, research and development, or security.
6. Legal Basis. The legal basis defines the criteria for obtaining the data. It can refer to the original contract (acceptance of the policy) or correspond to other sources such as legal or statutory obligations.
7. Personal data Disclosure specifies if the data will be shared with third parties referenced either by name or by category (e.g. payment providers).
8. Transfer to third countries or international organizations. This section lists the modalities of the transfers, including safeguards, adequacy decisions, and derogations.

9. Personal Data Retention. This section refers to the period of time during which the data will be kept, which can be indicated by a specific duration or a criterion.
10. Data Subjects Rights. This section lists various rights of the original data owner, such as access, rectification, or erasure.
11. Automated Decision-Making, including Profiling. This section refers to the modalities of automated decisions, such as the input data, output, and logic involved.
12. Personal Data Origin refers to the origin of the acquired data, which can, i.e., be directly acquired, provided by third parties, or publicly available.
13. Children. This section lists the data that is collected or not collected about children.
14. Personal Data Security refers to all measures that support data protection.

Annotations cover 40% of text length.

4.3 Task Definition

Like the authors of CUAD, we have associated each label sub-category with a question in order to train our question answering model. Examples of categories and question pairs are:

- *Category.* Transfer to third countries - Safeguards - Legally binding and enforceable instrument. *Question.* Is the transfer of data outside the European Economic Area supported by a legally binding and enforceable instrument between public authorities or bodies?
- *Category.* PD Data Retention - Criteria. *Question.* Are there criteria in order to determine the time storage of the data?
- *Category.* PD Origin - Indirect - Publicly. *Question.* Does the personal data processed come from a public source?
- *Category.* Processing Purposes - Research and development. *Question.* Is the information processed for research and development purposes?
- *Category.* Legal Basis - Legal obligation. *Question.* Is the data processing based on a legal obligation?

Answers were annotated at the span level, meaning that the exact words belonging to the answer are delimited by a starting and an ending token. Therefore, the answers are composed of excerpts from the privacy policies. For example, an answer to the question *Does the personal data processed come from a public source?* is *through publicly available records such as the electoral roll* (excerpt from the Binance privacy policy). An answer to the question *Is the information processed for a service provision purpose?* is *we publish statistical data on individual quickies in a summarized form* (excerpt from the Appinio privacy policy).

4.4 Labeling Process

GDPR120Q was created following a methodology very similar to that used by the authors of CUAD [34].

We started with a crowdsourcing phase, where the 120 policies were annotated multiple times by 150+ master students according to the conceptual model described in Sect. 4.2. The objective of this phase was to refine the task definition and to finalize the annotation instructions for the next phase. The students attended 28 h of training to learn how to label the privacy policies. The training included video instructions, live workshops with experienced lawyers, detailed instructions, and weekly follow-ups.

Each policy was then re-annotated by a group of three senior students who had 5 years of law training and were under the close supervision of three senior researchers and professors specialized in the field. This phase included weekly group meetings to clarify any remaining questions. Finally, the senior academics reviewed the annotated policies. The GDPR120Q dataset is among the few extensively annotated NLP benchmarks by specialists. Our aspiration is that this endeavor will not only support research on privacy compliance but also play a role in automating regulatory compliance.

The annotations were produced using the Ant annotation tool [29].

4.5 Limitations

GDPR120Q is a specialized dataset focusing on Document to Regulation compliance (defined in Sect. 2) under the European GDPR. The dataset encompasses eight industries: telecommunication, retail, entertainment, social networks, video games, health (excluding medical data), finance, and a broadly defined "service" category. Industries may be subject to additional regulations, such as those involving medical or health data, which are not reflected in this dataset.

5 Testing and Benchmarking GDPR120Q

In this section, we examine the outcomes of various tests conducted to benchmark GDPR120Q and to support the assertion that expert-annotated, domain-specific datasets are essential for developing innovative solutions in legal compliance.

5.1 Task Structure

Our task reuses the question-answering structure of SQuAD 2.0 [63], the current reference in the field of question answering. The same structure was also used for legal purposes by the authors of CUAD [34] as well as the authors of PolicyQA [3], who built a Q&A dataset that extends OPP-115 [83]. Question answering is a type of task frequently used in the legal field [1,14,22,24,35,37,42,51,53,72,89].

Our objective is to predict which parts of a privacy policy correspond to specific label categories by identifying all the annotated substrings belonging to that category. Each question specifies the label category being considered and is accompanied by answers indicating the corresponding parts of the context. During pre-processing, we generated unanswerable questions to test the ability of our models to detect these use cases. We then added these unanswerable questions to the corpus before training. Unanswerable questions are questions that belong to the task definition but that cannot be answered based on the context available to the model. For instance, a question like "Are there criteria for determining data storage duration?" would be unanswerable if the provided text discusses an unrelated topic, such as the identification of the controller or the DPO.

The code used for pre-processing and training the algorithms is available on GitHub[3].

5.2 Models

We evaluate the performance of BERT [23], RoBERTa [50] and DeBERTa [32,33]. BERT, RoBERTa, and DeBERTa are all variants of transformer-based neural network models designed for natural language processing tasks. Our purpose is to provide different baseline models that show that algorithms can learn the task.

BERT (Bidirectional Encoder Representations from Transformers) uses a bidirectional transformer encoder to pre-train the model on large amounts of unlabeled text data and then fine-tune it on a specific natural language processing task, such as question answering. Legal-BERT [19] reuses the architecture of BERT and pretrained the model on legal texts such as EU legislation and cases from the European Court of Justice. RoBERTa (Robustly Optimized BERT Pretraining Approach) is an optimized version of BERT. Its main contribution is to perform masking dynamically during training, not during preprocessing. RoBERTa achieved improved performance compared to BERT on several NLP tasks. LegalRoBERTa [26] is an adaptation of RoBERTa to the legal domain. DeBERTa (Decoding-enhanced BERT with Disentangled Attention) is a newer transformer-based neural network model introduced in 2020 by Microsoft Research. It extends the BERT architecture by introducing a disentangled attention mechanism that separates the learning of local and global dependencies in the input sequence. It also includes a decoding-enhanced architecture allowing better modeling of future contexts. DeBERTa has shown improved performance compared to BERT and RoBERTa on several NLP benchmarks [32,33].

We loaded pre-trained versions of these models from the HuggingFace Transformers library [84].

5.3 Training

We generate an 80/20 train test split using a multilabel data stratification algorithm [70] at the document level, in order to maintain a representative distribu-

[3] https://github.com/raphaelgyory/GDPR120Q.

tion of the various labels across the datasets. We then performed a second split of the train set during the pre-processing phase to obtain a validation set.

Model checkpoints and their parameters are available on zenodo.org[4]. To address long document lengths, we trained the models paragraph by paragraph. We trained the models on the entire training set and tested them on the entire test set.

5.4 Results

We used the metrics provided by the authors of CUAD [34] to evaluate our task, and used their script available on GitHub[5]. This script uses the Jaccard similarity coefficient to compute the overlap between the highlighted text and the ground truth.

The Jaccard similarity coefficient is defined as:

$$J(A,B) = \frac{|A \cap B|}{|A \cup B|} \tag{1}$$

where A is the set of words in an annotation, and B is the set of words in the prediction. This script does some text pre-processing by removing punctuation, putting the text in lower case and splitting string on white spaces. Like the authors of CUAD, we use the threshold $0.5 \leq J(A,B)$ for determining matches.

We show the results of the trained models in Table 2 as well as the precision-recall curves for three of these models in Fig. 2, which highlight the general behavior of the BERT model and its successors on our dataset as well as the trade-off between precision and recall. Figure 3 plots the area under the precision-recall curve for each main category of questions.

Table 2. Scores (micro) of the trained models on the GDPR120Q test set. Similar to the authors of CUAD, we assume that 80% recall "may already be reasonable for some lawyers" [34]. However, algorithms aimed at individuals will require a higher score.

Model	AUPR	Prec. at 80% rec.	Prec. at 90% rec.
bert-base-uncased	0.661	0.443	0.167
legal-bert-base-uncased	0.669	0.442	0.268
roberta-base	0.670	0.454	0.000
legal-roberta-base	0.664	0.458	0.000
deberta-v3-base	0.630	0.356	0.147
deberta-v3-large	0.661	0.431	0.000

4 https://zenodo.org/doi/10.5281/zenodo.10440240.

5 https://github.com/TheAtticusProject/cuad/blob/main/evaluate.py.

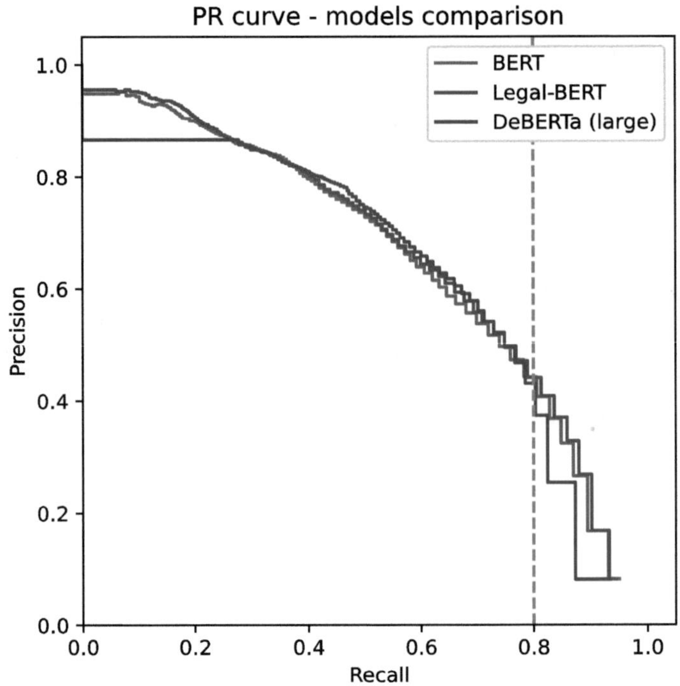

Fig. 2. The precision-recall curve for three baseline models. We loaded these models from HuggingFace [84]. This plot illustrates the trade-off between precision and recall.

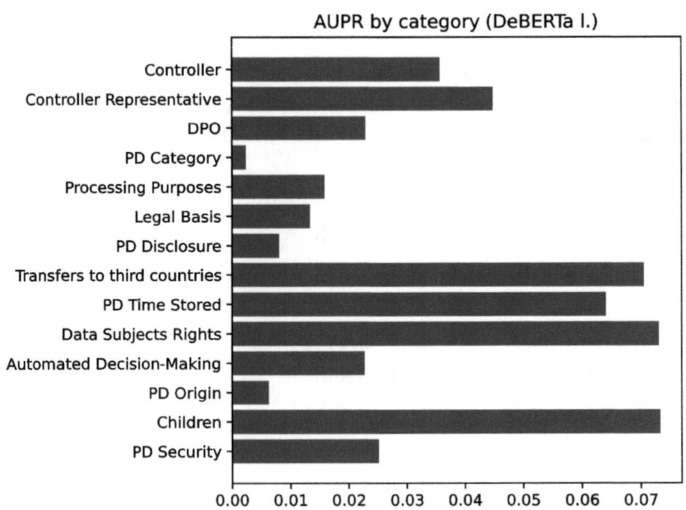

Fig. 3. The area under the precision-recall curve for each main category of questions, using the results of the DeBERTaV3 (large) model [32,33].

We then compare the results of a baseline BERT model trained on our dataset, a BERT model pretrained on the 130.000 policies of the Princeton Leuven dataset and a BERT model pretrained on the Princeton Leuven dataset and trained on our dataset (Fig. 4). This comparison underscores the value added by our annotation work, as the BERT model trained on our GDPR120Q dataset significantly outperforms the BERT model pretrained on the 130,000 policies of the Princeton Leuven dataset. Additionally, the BERT model pretrained on the Princeton Leuven dataset and then trained on GDPR120Q shows only marginal improvement over the BERT model trained solely on GDPR120Q.

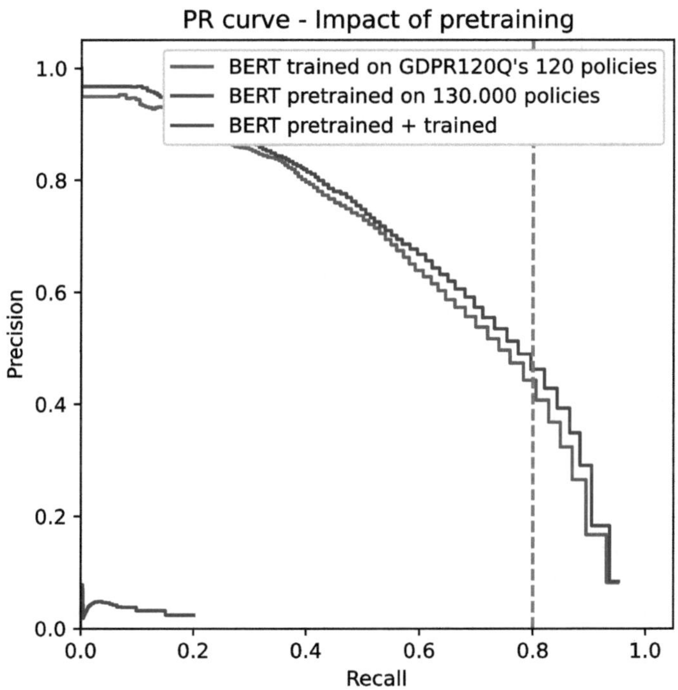

Fig. 4. Comparing the results of (1) a BERT model trained on our dataset, (2) a BERT model pretrained on the 130.000 policies of the Princeton Leuven dataset and (3) a BERT model pretrained on the Princeton Leuven dataset and trained on our dataset. This comparison underscores the added value of our annotations compared to simple pretraining on unannotated data.

To show the importance of having large amounts of annotated data, we trained the DeBERTa V3 model respectively on 1,000 annotations, 10,000 annotations, and the whole dataset. Figure 5 illustrates that the model performs better with more training data, highlighting the significance of high-quality training data, which is the primary focus of our research.

Finally, Fig. 6 offers a comparison of three BERT models trained respectively on the GDPR120Q (blue) training set, the OPP-115 based PolicyQA training

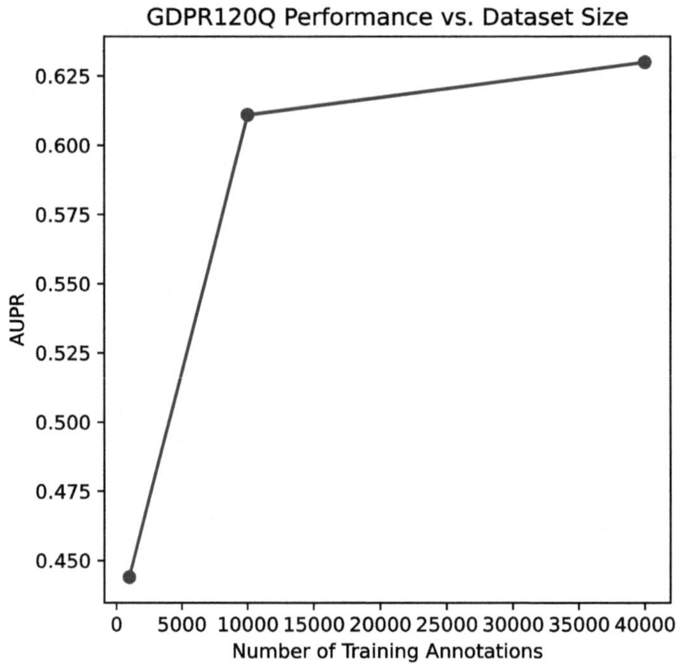

Fig. 5. The results of the DeBERTA V3 (base) model [32,33] trained respectively on 1,000 annotations, 10,000 annotations and the whole dataset. The plot shows the importance of having high quantities of high-quality training data to achieve sufficient model performance.

set (gray) and the CUAD training set (red) and tested on the GDPR120Q test set. These two datasets constitute the two Q&A tasks that are compatible with GDPR120Q. Figure 6 shows that GDPR120Q contains questions that these two non GDPR related tasks cannot answer.

5.5 GPT

Finally, we test GPT on our dataset. We use OpenAI's API and the *gpt-3.5-turbo* model parameterized with a temperature of 0, which aims at rendering the output more deterministic[6].

GPT is the most advanced LLM to date and has returned promising results on tasks such as taking or even passing bar exams [13,41], the American Institute of Certified Public Accountants' Uniform CPA Examination [13] as well as on ML tasks such as the COLIEE legal entailment task [87].

Evaluating the performance of GPT on an extractive Q&A task such as GDPR120Q is an uneasy task for three main reasons.

[6] https://platform.openai.com/docs/api-reference/completions.

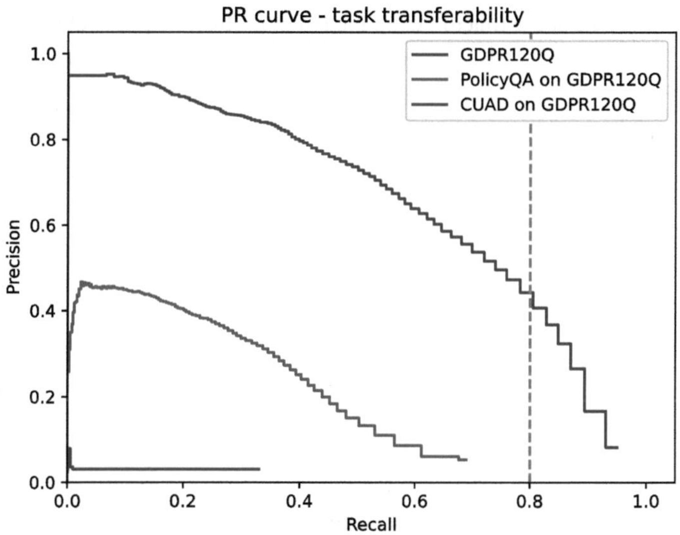

Fig. 6. The results of the two other related compatible Q&A tasks on the GDPR120Q test set. This plot highlights the specificity of our task, as models trained on other datasets are unable to answer GDPR120Q's questions accurately. (Color figure online)

First, GPT performs a different task than the BERT family of algorithms we used in the preceding section. GPT is a generative model with reasoning capabilities. It is closed source and cannot be fine-tuned by its users to perform extractive questions answering. Instead, GPT must be expressively instructed via a prompt to extract text spans, without generating extra content. Our experiences show that GPT can limit itself to extracting text but does not always do. For example, GPT may return answers such as *Yes. ("service provision purpose", "develop our relationship with you")*, instead of an array of separate responses. This behavior can add unstructured and unpredictable artifacts to the answers, potentially perturbing the evaluation of the task. To the best of our knowledge, there is no established methodology for evaluating two distinct tasks such as extractive Q&A and generative reasoning.

Secondly, questions are sent to GPT by means of a prompt. The question formulation has an impact on GPT's response [12,28,86]. The utilization of the prompt is currently an open question, and a variety of approaches are being analyzed by the research community, such as few-shot prompting, chain-of-thought prompting, and zero-shot prompting [12,13,67,87].

A third obstacle to decision making and document review automation is that GPT does not return the probabilities associated to its outputs. This prevents the use of metrics such as the precision-recall curve which ranks predictions and sweeps through different thresholds to compute precision and recall at each threshold.

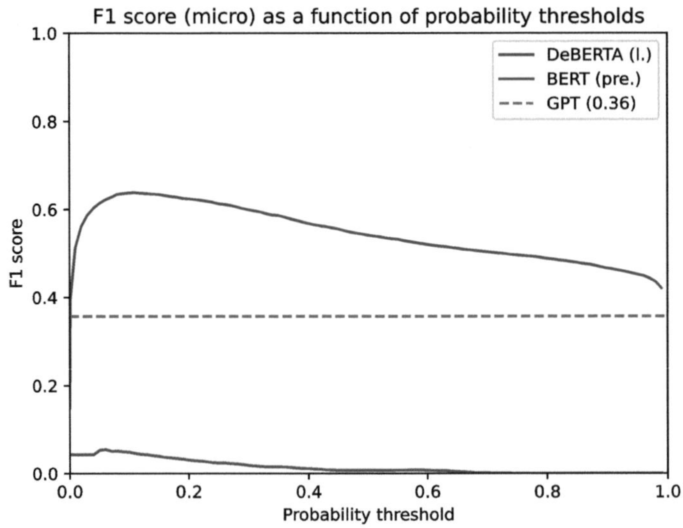

Fig. 7. Comparison of the trained DeBERTa V3 model, the pretrained only BERT model and GPT3. GPT results are denoted by a dashed line, because GPT does not return probability thresholds.

Figure 7 shows the F1 score at different probability thresholds for the trained DeBERTa V3 models and the pretrained only BERT model. Trained baseline models outperformed GPT3 for most thresholds. These scores suggest that our task, which requires specialized domain expertise, cannot be fully delegated to LLMs and is in line with other studies [12,17,36,47,56]. This graph shows, however, that GPT represents a considerable advance over models with pretraining alone, in this case BERT.

These limitations do not prevent GPT from being a promising tool for privacy compliance tasks. An interesting solution that is emerging in the research consists in leveraging these models to support the work of annotators [27,61,90]. This solution offers the dual advantage of helping to extend LLM research, while facilitating the production of benchmarks at the same time. At the time of writing, the potential assistance this model offers in the annotation process of privacy data appears promising but falls short of being a definitive solution for our task. Further research is necessary to determine whether, and in what ways, it can effectively support annotators or if its utility will remain only marginal in the annotation process of privacy data under the GDPR.

6 Conclusion

Ensuring compliance with data privacy regulations and policies is a challenge in the evolving digital economy. Document-to-regulation compliance, especially within global data supply chains, is notably challenging, time-intensive and costly. In this paper, we have argued that NLLP using deep learning techniques could be a valuable component in achieving automated compliance, provided that there is access to comprehensive, domain-specific labeled datasets.

In this context, we introduced GDPR120Q, the first large-scale open-source annotated dataset for GDPR compliance consisting of 39,834 Q&A annotations by legal experts. We evaluated several pre-trained language models on GDPR120Q and showed that the dataset contributes significantly to improving performance for document-to-regulation compliance tasks. The substantial volume of annotations in GDPR120Q appears critical, as a reduction in data volume significantly impacts performance.

Although there remains considerable room for improvement, GDPR120Q marks a breakthrough in the field of document-to-regulation privacy compliance. It holds the potential to significantly contribute to research towards automated GDPR compliance. It can also serve as a benchmark for assessing NLLP models for privacy compliance more broadly.

Disclosure of Interests. The authors have no competing interests to declare that are relevant to the content of this article.

References

1. Abdallah, A., Piryani, B., Jatowt, A.: Exploring the state of the art in legal QA systems. J. Big. Data. **10**(1), 127 (2023). https://doi.org/10.1186/s40537-023-00802-8
2. Ahmad, W., Chi, J., Le, T., Norton, T., Tian, Y., Chang, K.W.: Intent classification and slot filling for privacy policies. In: Proceedings of the 59th Annual Meeting of the Association for Computational Linguistics and the 11th International Joint Conference on Natural Language Processing, Online, vol. 1, pp. 4402–4417. Association for Computational Linguistics (2021). https://doi.org/10.18653/v1/2021.acl-long.340. https://aclanthology.org/2021.acl-long.340
3. Ahmad, W., Chi, J., Tian, Y., Chang, K.W.: PolicyQA: a reading comprehension dataset for privacy policies. In: Findings of the Association for Computational Linguistics: EMNLP 2020, Online, pp. 743–749. Association for Computational Linguistics (2020). https://doi.org/10.18653/v1/2020.findings-emnlp.66. https://aclanthology.org/2020.findings-emnlp.66
4. Ahmed, J., Yildirim, S., Nowostawski, M., Abomhara, M., Ramachandra, R., Elezaj, O.: Towards blockchain-based GDPR-compliant online social networks: challenges, opportunities and way forward. In: Arai, K., Kapoor, S., Bhatia, R. (eds.) Advances in Information and Communication, pp. 113–129. Springer, Cham (2020)
5. Alabduljabbar, A., Abusnaina, A., Meteriz-Yildiran, U., Mohaisen, D.: Automated privacy policy annotation with information highlighting made practical using deep representations. In: Proceedings of the 2021 ACM SIGSAC Conference on Computer and Communications Security, pp. 2378–2380. ACM, Virtual Event, Republic of Korea (2021). https://doi.org/10.1145/3460120.3485335. https://dl.acm.org/doi/10.1145/3460120.3485335

6. Almeida Teixeira, G., Mira da Silva, M., Pereira, R.: The critical success factors of GDPR implementation: a systematic literature review. Digit. Pol. Regul. Gov. **21**(4), 402–418 (2019)
7. Amaral, O., Abualhaija, S., Torre, D., Sabetzadeh, M., Briand, L.C.: AI-enabled automation for completeness checking of privacy policies. IEEE Trans. Softw. Eng. **48**(11), 4647–4674 (2022). https://doi.org/10.1109/TSE.2021.3124332
8. Amariles, D.R., Troussel, A.C., Hamdani, R.E.: Compliance generation for privacy documents under GDPR: a roadmap for implementing automation and machine learning. arXiv preprint arXiv:2012.12718 (2020)
9. Amos, R., Acar, G., Lucherini, E., Kshirsagar, M., Narayanan, A., Mayer, J.: Privacy policies over time: curation and analysis of a million-document dataset. In: Proceedings of the Web Conference, pp. 2165–2176 (2021). https://doi.org/10.1145/3442381.3450048. http://arxiv.org/abs/2008.09159. arXiv arXiv:2008.09159
10. Audich, D.A., Dara, R., Nonnecke, B.: Privacy policy annotation for semi-automated analysis: a cost-effective approach. In: Gal-Oz, N., Lewis, P.R. (eds.) IFIPTM 2018. IAICT, vol. 528, pp. 29–44. Springer, Cham (2018). https://doi.org/10.1007/978-3-319-95276-5_3
11. Bannihatti Kumar, V., et al.: Finding a choice in a haystack: automatic extraction of opt-out statements from privacy policy text. In: Proceedings of the Web Conference 2020, pp. 1943–1954 (2020)
12. Blair-Stanek, A., Holzenberger, N., Van Durme, B.: Can GPT-3 perform statutory reasoning? In: Proceedings of the Nineteenth International Conference on Artificial Intelligence and Law, ICAIL 2023, pp. 22–31. Association for Computing Machinery, New York (2023). https://doi.org/10.1145/3594536.3595163
13. Bommarito, J., Bommarito, M., Katz, D.M., Katz, J.: GPT as knowledge worker: a zero-shot evaluation of (AI)CPA capabilities. Technical report. arXiv arXiv:2301.04408, January 2023. http://arxiv.org/abs/2301.04408
14. Bongard, L., Held, L., Habernal, I.: The legal argument reasoning task in civil procedure. In: Proceedings of the Natural Legal Language Processing Workshop 2022, pp. 194–207. Association for Computational Linguistics 2022, December 2022. pp. 194–207. Association for Computational Linguistics (2022). https://doi.org/10.18653/v1/2022.nllp-1.17. https://aclanthology.org/2022.nllp-1.17D
15. Bui, D., Shin, K.G., Choi, J.M., Shin, J.: Automated extraction and presentation of data practices in privacy policies. Proc. Priv. Enhancing Technol. **2021**(2), 88–110 (2021). https://doi.org/10.2478/popets-2021-0019. https://doi.org/10.2478/popets-2021-0019
16. Cejas, O.A., Azeem, M.I., Abualhaija, S., Briand, L.C.: NLP-based automated compliance checking of data processing agreements against GDPR. IEEE Trans. Softw. Eng. **49**(09), 4282–4303 (2023). https://doi.org/10.1109/TSE.2023.3288901. https://doi.ieeecomputersociety.org/10.1109/TSE.2023.3288901
17. Chalkidis, I.: ChatGPT may pass the bar exam soon, but has a long way to go for the LexGLUE benchmark. Technical report. arXiv arXiv:2304.12202 (2023). http://arxiv.org/abs/2304.12202
18. Chalkidis, I., Androutsopoulos, I., Michos, A.: Extracting contract elements. In: Proceedings of the 16th Edition of the International Conference on Articial Intelligence and Law, pp. 19–28 (2017)
19. Chalkidis, I., Fergadiotis, M., Malakasiotis, P., Aletras, N., Androutsopoulos, I.: LEGAL-BERT: the muppets straight out of law school. In: Findings of the Association for Computational Linguistics, EMNLP 2020, Online, pp. 2898–2904. Association for Computational Linguistics (2020). https://doi.org/10.18653/v1/2020.findings-emnlp.261. https://aclanthology.org/2020.findings-emnlp.261

20. Chander, A., Abraham, M., Chandy, S., Fang, Y., Park, D., Yu, I.: Achieving privacy: costs of compliance and enforcement of data protection regulation. Policy Res. Working Pap. **9594** (2021)
21. Chen, C., Frey, C.B., Presidente, G.: Privacy regulation and firm performance: estimating the GDPR effect globally. Technical report, The Oxford Martin Working Paper Series on Technological and Economic Change (2022)
22. Collarana, D., et al.: A question answering system on regulatory documents. In: Legal Knowledge and Information Systems, pp. 41–50. IOS Press (2018). https://doi.org/10.3233/978-1-61499-935-5-41. https://ebooks.iospress.nl/doi/10.3233/978-1-61499-935-5-41
23. Devlin, J., Chang, M.W., Lee, K., Toutanova, K.: BERT: pre-training of deep bidirectional transformers for language understanding. In: Proceedings of the 2019 Conference of the North American Chapter of the Association for Computational Linguistics: Human Language Technologies, Minneapolis, Minnesota, vol. 1, pp. 4171–4186. Association for Computational Linguistics (2019). https://doi.org/10.18653/v1/N19-1423. https://aclanthology.org/N19-1423
24. Duan, X., et al.: CJRC: a reliable human-annotated benchmark dataset for Chinese judicial reading comprehension. In: Sun, M., Huang, X., Ji, H., Liu, Z., Liu, Y. (eds.) CCL 2019. LNCS (LNAI), vol. 11856, pp. 439–451. Springer, Cham (2019). https://doi.org/10.1007/978-3-030-32381-3_36
25. Fazlioglu, M.: IAPP-EY annual privacy governance report 2021. IAPP Report (2021). https://papers.ssrn.com/sol3/papers.cfm?abstract_id=4227244. Accessed 5 Sept 2023
26. Geng, S., Lebret, R., Aberer, K.: Legal transformer models may not always help. arXiv preprint arXiv:2109.06862 (2021)
27. Gilardi, F., Alizadeh, M., Kubli, M.: ChatGPT outperforms crowd workers for text-annotation tasks. Proc. Natl. Acad. Sci. U.S.A. **120**(30), e2305016120 (2023). https://doi.org/10.1073/pnas.2305016120
28. Goodhue, J., Wei, Y.: Classification of trademark distinctiveness using OpenAI GPT 3.5 model. SSRN Electron. J. (2023). https://doi.org/10.2139/ssrn.4351998. https://www.ssrn.com/abstract=4351998
29. Gyory, R., Restrepo Amariles, D., Lewkowicz, G., Bersini, H.: Ant: a process aware annotation software for regulatory compliance. Artif. Intell. Law (2023). https://doi.org/10.1007/s10506-023-09372-9
30. Hamdani, R.E., Mustapha, M., Amariles, D.R., Troussel, A., Meeùs, S., Krasnashchok, K.: A combined rule-based and machine learning approach for automated GDPR compliance checking. In: Proceedings of the Eighteenth International Conference on Artificial Intelligence and Law, São Paulo, Brazil, pp. 40–49. ACM (2021). https://doi.org/10.1145/3462757.3466081. https://dl.acm.org/doi/10.1145/3462757.3466081
31. Harkous, H., Fawaz, K., Lebret, R., Schaub, F., Shin, K.G., Aberer, K.: Polisis: automated analysis and presentation of privacy policies using deep learning. In: Proceedings of the 27th USENIX Conference on Security Symposium, SEC'18, Baltimore, MD, USA, pp. 531–548. USENIX Association, USA (2018)
32. He, P., Gao, J., Chen, W.: DeBERTaV3: improving DeBERTa using ELECTRA-style pre-training with gradient-disentangled embedding sharing. arXiv arXiv:2111.09543 (2021)
33. He, P., Liu, X., Gao, J., Chen, W.: DeBERTa: decoding-enhanced BERT with disentangled attention. In: International Conference on Learning Representations (2021). https://openreview.net/forum?id=XPZIaotutsD

34. Hendrycks, D., Burns, C., Chen, A., Ball, S.: CUAD: an expert-annotated NLP dataset for legal contract review. In: Vanschoren, J., Yeung, S. (eds.) Proceedings of the Neural Information Processing Systems Track on Datasets and Benchmarks, vol. 1 (2021). https://datasets-benchmarks-proceedings.neurips.cc/paper_files/paper/2021/file/6ea9ab1baa0efb9e19094440c317e21b-Paper-round1.pdf
35. Hoppe, C., Pelkmann, D., Migenda, N., Hötte, D., Schenck, W.: Towards intelligent legal advisors for document retrieval and question-answering in German legal documents. In: 2021 IEEE Fourth International Conference on Artificial Intelligence and Knowledge Engineering (AIKE), pp. 29–32. IEEE (2021)
36. Huang, F., Kwak, H., An, J.: Is ChatGPT better than human annotators? Potential and limitations of ChatGPT in explaining implicit hate speech. In: Companion Proceedings of the ACM Web Conference 2023, April 2023, pp. 294–297 (2023). https://doi.org/10.1145/3543873.3587368. http://arxiv.org/abs/2302.07736. arXiv arXiv:2302.07736 [cs]
37. Huang, W., Jiang, J., Qu, Q., Yang, M.: AILA: a question answering system in the legal domain. In: IJCAI, pp. 5258–5260 (2020)
38. Ponemon Institute: Keeping Pace in the GDPR Race (2019). https://www.privacysecurityacademy.com/wp-content/uploads/2019/06/Keeping-Pace-in-the-GDPR-Race.pdf. Accessed 5 May 2023
39. Johansson, E., Sutinen, K., Lassila, J., Lang, V., Martikainen, M., Lehner, O.M.: RegTech-a necessary tool to keep up with compliance and regulatory changes. ACRN J. Financ. Risk Perspect. Spec. Issue Digit. Account. **8**, 71–85 (2019)
40. Johnson, J.: GDPR: implementation cost by sector 2018 Statistic (2018). https://www.statista.com/statistics/869613/gdpr-implementation-cost-by-sector/. Accessed 5 May 2023
41. Katz, D.M., Bommarito, M.J., Gao, S., Arredondo, P.: GPT-4 passes the bar exam. Philos. Trans. Ser. A Math. Phys. Eng. Sci. **382**(2270), 20230254 (2024). https://doi.org/10.1098/rsta.2023.0254
42. Kim, M.Y., Goebel, R., Ken, S.: COLIEE-2015: evaluation of legal question answering. In: Ninth International Workshop on Juris-Informatics, JURISIN 2015 (2015)
43. Koreeda, Y., Manning, C.: ContractNLI: a dataset for document-level natural language inference for contracts. In: Moens, M.F., Huang, X., Specia, L., Yih, S.W. (eds.) Findings of the Association for Computational Linguistics, EMNLP 2021, Punta Cana, Dominican Republic, November 2021, pp. 1907–1919. Association for Computational Linguistics (2021). https://doi.org/10.18653/v1/2021.findings-emnlp.164. https://aclanthology.org/2021.findings-emnlp.164
44. Lee, G.E., Sun, A.: A study on agreement in PICO span annotations. In: Proceedings of the 42nd International ACM SIGIR Conference on Research and Development in Information Retrieval, July 2019, pp. 1149–1152 (2018). https://doi.org/10.1145/3331184.3331352. http://arxiv.org/abs/1904.09557. arXiv arXiv:1904.09557 [cs]
45. Leivaditi, S., Rossi, J., Kanoulas, E.: A benchmark for lease contract review. arXiv preprint arXiv:2010.10386 (2020)
46. Leonelli, S.: Data—from objects to assets. Nature **574**(7778), 317–320 (2019). bandiera_abtest: a Cg_type: Comment Number: 7778. https://doi.org/10.1038/d41586-019-03062-w. https://www.nature.com/articles/d41586-019-03062-w
47. Li, X., et al.: Are ChatGPT and GPT-4 general-purpose solvers for financial text analytics? A study on several typical tasks. In: Wang, M., Zitouni, I. (eds.) Proceedings of the 2023 Conference on Empirical Methods in Natural Language Processing: Industry Track, December 2023, pp. 408–422. Association for Computational

Linguistics, Singapore (2023). https://doi.org/10.18653/v1/2023.emnlp-industry.39. https://aclanthology.org/2023.emnlp-industry.39
48. Li, Z.S., Werner, C., Ernst, N., Damian, D.: Towards privacy compliance: a design science study in a small organization. Inf. Softw. Technol. **146**, 106868 (2022). https://doi.org/10.1016/j.infsof.2022.106868. https://www.sciencedirect.com/science/article/pii/S0950584922000362
49. Lippi, M., et al.: CLAUDETTE: an automated detector of potentially unfair clauses in online terms of service. Artif. Intell. Law **27**, 117–139 (2019)
50. Liu, Y., et al.: RoBERTa: a robustly optimized BERT pretraining approach. arXiv preprint arXiv:1907.11692 (2019)
51. Louis, A., Spanakis, G.: A statutory article retrieval dataset in French. In: Muresan, S., Nakov, P., Villavicencio, A. (eds.) Proceedings of the 60th Annual Meeting of the Association for Computational Linguistics (Volume 1: Long Papers), Dublin, Ireland, May 2022, pp. 6789–6803. Association for Computational Linguistics (2022). https://doi.org/10.18653/v1/2022.acl-long.468. https://aclanthology.org/2022.acl-long.468
52. Madden, M., Rainie, L.: Americans' attitudes about privacy, security and surveillance. Internet Sci. Tech. (2015). https://policycommons.net/artifacts/619110/americans-attitudes-about-privacy-security-and-surveillance/1600177/
53. Martinez-Gil, J., Freudenthaler, B., Tjoa, A.M.: Multiple choice question answering in the legal domain using reinforced co-occurrence. In: Hartmann, S., Küng, J., Chakravarthy, S., Anderst-Kotsis, G., Tjoa, A.M., Khalil, I. (eds.) Database and Expert Systems Applications, pp. 138–148. Springer, Cham (2019)
54. McDonald, A.M., Cranor, L.F.: The cost of reading privacy policies. ISJLP **4**, 543 (2008)
55. Meeùs, S.: Mandatory information under GDPR: a conceptual model for automated privacy policy analysis. In: Time to Reshape the Digital Society: 40th anniversary of the CRIDS, pp. 115–133. No. 52 in Collection du CRIDS, Larcier. Larcier (2021)
56. Nguyen, H.T., Goebel, R., Toni, F., Stathis, K., Satoh, K.: How well do SOTA legal reasoning models support abductive reasoning? Technical report. arXiv arXiv:2304.06912 [cs], April 2023. http://arxiv.org/abs/2304.06912
57. Nokhbeh Zaeem, R., Barber, K.S.: A large publicly available corpus of website privacy policies based on DMOZ. In: Proceedings of the Eleventh ACM Conference on Data and Application Security and Privacy, Virtual Event USA, April 2021, pp. 143–148. ACM (2021). https://doi.org/10.1145/3422337.3447827. https://dl.acm.org/doi/10.1145/3422337.3447827
58. Nye, B., Jessy Li, J., Patel, R., Yang, Y., Marshall, I.J., Nenkova, A., Wallace, B.C.: A corpus with multi-level annotations of patients, interventions and outcomes to support language processing for medical literature. In: Proceedings of the conference. Association for Computational Linguistics. Meeting, July 2018, vol. 2018, pp. 197–207 (2018). https://www.ncbi.nlm.nih.gov/pmc/articles/PMC6174533/
59. Obar, J.A., Oeldorf-Hirsch, A.: The biggest lie on the Internet: ignoring the privacy policies and terms of service policies of social networking services. Inf. Commun. Soc. **23**(1), 128–147 (2020). https://doi.org/10.1080/1369118X.2018.1486870
60. Pandit, H.J., et al.: Creating a vocabulary for data privacy: the first-year report of data privacy vocabularies and controls community group (DPVCG). In: On the Move to Meaningful Internet Systems: OTM 2019 Conferences: Confederated International Conferences: CoopIS, ODBASE, C&TC 2019, Rhodes, Greece, 21–25 October 2019, Proceedings, pp. 714–730. Springer, Heidelberg (2019)
61. Pangakis, N., Wolken, S., Fasching, N.: Automated annotation with generative AI requires validation (2023). https://arxiv.org/abs/2306.00176

62. Qamar, A., Javed, T., Beg, M.O.: Detecting compliance of privacy policies with data protection laws. Technical report. arXiv arXiv:2102.12362 [cs], February 2021. http://arxiv.org/abs/2102.12362
63. Rajpurkar, P., Jia, R., Liang, P.: Know what you don't know: unanswerable questions for SQuAD. In: Gurevych, I., Miyao, Y. (eds.) Proceedings of the 56th Annual Meeting of the Association for Computational Linguistics (Volume 2: Short Papers), Melbourne, Australia, July 2018, pp. 784–789. Association for Computational Linguistics (2018). https://doi.org/10.18653/v1/P18-2124
64. Rambaud, S.C., Gázquez, A.E.: A RegTech approach to Fintech sustainability: the case of Spain. Eur. J. Risk Regul. **13**(2), 333–349 (2022). https://doi.org/10.1017/err.2021.62. https://www.cambridge.org/core/journals/european-journal-of-risk-regulation/article/regtech-approach-to-fintech-sustainability-the-case-of-spain/8441E185FBCCF8117D363505C20871C8
65. Ravichander, A., Black, A.W., Wilson, S., Norton, T., Sadeh, N.: Question answering for privacy policies: combining computational and legal perspectives. In: Inui, K., Jiang, J., Ng, V., Wan, X. (eds.) Proceedings of the 2019 Conference on Empirical Methods in Natural Language Processing and the 9th International Joint Conference on Natural Language Processing (EMNLP-IJCNLP), Hong Kong, China, November 2019, pp. 4947–4958. Association for Computational Linguistics (2019). https://doi.org/10.18653/v1/D19-1500. https://aclanthology.org/D19-1500
66. Sathyendra, K.M., Wilson, S., Schaub, F., Zimmeck, S., Sadeh, N.: Identifying the provision of choices in privacy policy text. In: Proceedings of the 2017 Conference on Empirical Methods in Natural Language Processing, pp. 2774–2779 (2017)
67. Savelka, J.: Unlocking practical applications in legal domain: evaluation of GPT for zero-shot semantic annotation of legal texts. In: Proceedings of the Nineteenth International Conference on Artificial Intelligence and Law, ICAIL 2023, Braga, Portugal, pp. 447–451. Association for Computing Machinery, New York (2023). https://doi.org/10.1145/3594536.3595161
68. Schaub, F., Balebako, R., Cranor, L.F.: Designing effective privacy notices and controls. IEEE Internet Comput. **21**(3), 70–77 (2017). https://doi.org/10.1109/MIC.2017.75
69. Schwartz, P.M.: Property, privacy, and personal data. Harv. L. Rev. **117**, 2056 (2003)
70. Sechidis, K., Tsoumakas, G., Vlahavas, I.: On the stratification of multi-label data. In: Machine Learning and Knowledge Discovery in Databases: European Conference, ECML PKDD 2011, Proceedings, Part III 22, Athens, Greece, 5–9 September 2011, pp. 145–158. Springer, Heidelberg (2011)
71. Shvartzshnaider, Y., Apthorpe, N., Feamster, N., Nissenbaum, H.: Analyzing privacy policies using contextual integrity annotations. Technical report. arXiv arXiv:1809.02236 [cs], September 2018. http://arxiv.org/abs/1809.02236
72. Sovrano, F., Palmirani, M., Distefano, B., Sapienza, S., Vitali, F.: A dataset for evaluating legal question answering on private international law. In: Proceedings of the Eighteenth International Conference on Artificial Intelligence and Law, pp. 230–234 (2021)
73. Srinath, M., Wilson, S., Giles, C.L.: Privacy at scale: introducing the PrivaSeer Corpus of web privacy policies. In: Proceedings of the 59th Annual Meeting of the Association for Computational Linguistics and the 11th International Joint Conference on Natural Language Processing (Volume 1: Long Papers), Online, August 2021, pp. 6829–6839. Association for Computational Linguistics (2021). https://doi.org/10.18653/v1/2021.acl-long.532. https://aclanthology.org/2021.acl-long.532

74. Stourm, V., et al.: Refocusing loyalty programs in the era of Big Data: a societal lens paradigm. Market. Lett. **31**(4), 405–418 (2020). https://doi.org/10.1007/s11002-020-09523-x
75. Tesfay, W.B., Hofmann, P., Nakamura, T., Kiyomoto, S., Serna, J.: I read but don't agree: privacy policy benchmarking using machine learning and the EU GDPR. In: Companion of the The Web Conference 2018 on The Web Conference 2018, WWW '18, Lyon, France, pp. 163–166. ACM Press (2018). https://doi.org/10.1145/3184558.3186969. http://dl.acm.org/citation.cfm?doid=3184558.3186969
76. Torre, D., et al.: An AI-assisted approach for checking the completeness of privacy policies against GDPR. In: 2020 IEEE 28th International Requirements Engineering Conference (RE), pp. 136–146. IEEE (2020)
77. Torre, D., Alferez, M., Soltana, G., Sabetzadeh, M., Briand, L.: Modeling data protection and privacy: application and experience with GDPR. Softw. Syst. Model. **20**(6), 2071–2087 (2021). https://doi.org/10.1007/s10270-021-00935-5
78. Tuggener, D., von Däniken, P., Peetz, T., Cieliebak, M.: LEDGAR: a large-scale multi-label corpus for text classification of legal provisions in contracts. In: Proceedings of the Twelfth Language Resources and Evaluation Conference, Marseille, France, May 2020, pp. 1235–1241. European Language Resources Association (2020). https://aclanthology.org/2020.lrec-1.155
79. Villata, S., et al.: Thirty years of artificial intelligence and law: the third decade. Artif. Intell. Law **30**(4), 561–591 (2022). https://doi.org/10.1007/s10506-022-09327-6
80. Wachter, S.: Normative challenges of identification in the Internet of Things: privacy, profiling, discrimination, and the GDPR. Comput. Law Secur. Rev. **34**(3), 436–449 (2018). https://doi.org/10.1016/j.clsr.2018.02.002. https://www.sciencedirect.com/science/article/pii/S0267364917303904
81. Wagner, I.: Privacy policies across the ages: content of privacy policies 1996–2021. ACM Trans. Priv. Secur., 3590152 (2023). https://doi.org/10.1145/3590152. https://dl.acm.org/doi/10.1145/3590152
82. Wang, S., et al.: MAUD: an expert-annotated legal NLP dataset for merger agreement understanding. In: Bouamor, H., Pino, J., Bali, K. (eds.) Proceedings of the 2023 Conference on Empirical Methods in Natural Language Processing, Singapore, December 2023, pp. 16369–16382. Association for Computational Linguistics (2023). https://doi.org/10.18653/v1/2023.emnlp-main.1019
83. Wilson, S., et al.: The creation and analysis of a website privacy policy corpus. In: Proceedings of the 54th Annual Meeting of the Association for Computational Linguistics (Volume 1: Long Papers), Berlin, Germany, pp. 1330–1340. Association for Computational Linguistics (2016). https://doi.org/10.18653/v1/P16-1126. http://aclweb.org/anthology/P16-1126
84. Wolf, T., et al.: Transformers: state-of-the-art natural language processing. In: Proceedings of the 2020 Conference on Empirical Methods in Natural Language Processing: System Demonstrations, pp. 38–45 (2020)
85. Wolff, J., Atallah, N.: Early GDPR penalties: analysis of implementation and fines through May 2020. J. Inf. Policy **11**, 63–103 (2021). https://doi.org/10.5325/jinfopoli.11.2021.0063
86. Xu, B., et al.: ExpertPrompting: instructing large language models to be distinguished experts. Technical report. arXiv arXiv:2305.14688 [cs], May 2023
87. Yu, F., Quartey, L., Schilder, F.: Legal prompting: teaching a language model to think like a lawyer. Technical report. arXiv arXiv:2212.01326 [cs], December 2022. http://arxiv.org/abs/2212.01326

88. Zaman, R., Hassani, M.: On enabling GDPR compliance in business processes through data-driven solutions. SN Comput. Sci. **1**(4), 210 (2020)
89. Zhong, H., Xiao, C., Tu, C., Zhang, T., Liu, Z., Sun, M.: JEC-QA: a legal-domain question answering dataset. In: Proceedings of the AAAI Conference on Artificial Intelligence, vol. 34, no. 05, pp. 9701–9708 (2020)
90. Zhu, Y., Zhang, P., Haq, E.U., Hui, P., Tyson, G.: Can ChatGPT reproduce human-generated labels? A study of social computing tasks. Technical report. arXiv arXiv:2304.10145 [cs], April 2023. http://arxiv.org/abs/2304.10145
91. Zimmeck, S., et al.: MAPS: scaling privacy compliance analysis to a million apps. Proc. Priv. Enhancing Technol. **2019**(3), 66–86 (2019)

Automated Variance in Legal Decision-Making

Damien Charlotin(✉)

HEC Paris, Jouy-en-Josas, France
damien.charlotin@gmail.com

Abstract. The deployment of machine learning methods and artificial intelligence in the context of legal decision-making will require a thorough look at the concept of variance–be it that original to human decision-makers, or that of automated systems. Human judges are, indeed, noisy in their decisions, a fact that, though deplorable from the viewpoint of individual cases, may have systemic value for the legal framework as a whole: individual variance in legal cases functions as an information-collection device that propagates, throughout the legal system, a potential lack of fit between a norm and its application, and calls for a resolution. Besides, in justice as in machine learning, randomness and variance are, increasingly, not merely a byproduct but a fundamental feature that enables these systems to avoid being trapped in sub-optimal configurations. In this context, this Note offers some reflections on whether algorithmic methods should seek to suppress or replicate variance in legal decision-making, and what principles should govern any deployment of deliberate, automated variance.

Keywords: AI · Variance · Legal Decision-Making

1 Introduction

The progress of Artificial Intelligence (AI) has made all the more urgent a reflection about the role and scope of automated decision-making. The replacement of judges by algorithms or robots is not a question of whether, but of when - and that when is now in the past, as legal systems the world over have opted to automate some parts of their decision-making apparatus, or to provide judges with AI legal assistants on some discrete matters. This automation currently covers small claims such as speeding tickets; procedural issues such as bail applications [12]; assistance in sentencing guidelines [15]; or even the automatic treatment of administrative requests. In some fields, such as privacy law, automation is now even required by some legal frameworks to ensure compliance [17].

Amongst the principles that govern the application of a legal system to real-world problems and disputes, one stands to be particularly affected by automated justice: the idea that, all things otherwise equal, the same cases or situations should be treated the same. In other words, a legal input, facing an unchanged

© The Author(s), under exclusive license to Springer Nature Switzerland AG 2026
D. Restrepo Amariles and K. Satoh (Eds.): *Compliance for Artificial Intelligence Systems*, LNAI 14377, pp. 49–58, 2026.
https://doi.org/10.1007/978-3-032-12795-2_4

legal framework, should correspond to an invariable legal output. This intuition underpins countless legal concepts, some as fundamental as the rule of law, but also institutional devices such as *stare decisis* in some legal systems, or the distinction between various types of precedents (*ratio*, *obiter dicta*, etc.). More generally, the attention given by legislators, lawyers, and judges to the consistency and predictability of the law partakes in the fundamental idea that likes should be treated alike.

And yet, amongst the profound discrepancies between the theory of the law and its practice, this principle is frequently disregarded. Be it due to evolving societal norms, the peculiarities of individual cases, or the interpretative lenses of different jurists, the law *is* routinely applied differently in comparable cases. While many of these discrepancies are not remedied (i.e., when a "wrong" case is not appealed), others are also sometimes celebrated (i.e., when a "wrong" precedent is overturned). Without always acknowledging it as such, legal systems have developed ways to cope with the consequences of variance, either to justify it (e.g., theories of "living law", expectations that the law should evolve with new circumstances), or to moderate it (e.g., through a hierarchical judicial system).

This has made variance an important entry point into the intricacies of a legal system, but is also an important underlying concern in discussions about AI and law: whereas the invariance of automated legal decision-making is one of the key advantages of these approaches (in comparison with noisy human judges), it has rarely been noted that there could be room for automated variance. For instance, through mechanisms such as temperature settings in generative models, it is now conceivable to introduce a controlled degree of variability in algorithmic outputs, mirroring, to some extent, the human capacity for discretion and adaptation. This deliberate variance, however, comes with important concerns that touch upon the very foundations of a legal system in terms of trust and legitimacy.

This Note will thus seek to chart the manifestations of variance in both legal and algorithmic contexts, and to examine the implications of this variance for the integrity and efficacy of legal systems. Focusing on "judicial" decision-making (although there is also variance at various stages of the legal chain), this Note will seek to articulate a balanced approach to the incorporation of variance in legal AI systems–an approach that recognizes the value of consistency and predictability in upholding the rule of law, while also acknowledging the potential of judiciously-applied variance in fostering the development of jurisprudence, and in tailoring justice to the varying circumstances of human life.

2 Variance in the Legal Field

Variance in Legal Cases. While ubiquitous and long-standing, the practice of resolving disputes through a third party, including disputes that pertain to the application of a communal norm, is far from a perfect system [1]. A fundamental issue in this process is also what is often valued as its greater strength: and the idea that skilled humans will review a case on its own merits. One particular type of humans, jurists, bring to the bench their unique amalgamation of professional experiences, personal convictions, and jurisprudential philosophies, all sources of deviations from the norm. The broad spectrum of legal philosophies–from strict textualism to groundless interpretivism–shapes jurists' approach to the interpretation of laws and precedents, and their willingness to strike their own way.

Beyond the legal framework, personal biases and cultural backgrounds, consciously or not, further infuse judicial reasoning with a level of subjectivity. While bias should not be confused with variance at the individual level, subjectivity at the system level is bound to introduce variability into legal decisions, jeopardizing the uniformity and predictability of legal outcomes.

Such variance is not merely theoretical, but has been demonstrated again and again in various contexts. Multiple analyses have demonstrated that asylum judges, for instance, have high variance in deciding cases for no good (i.e., legally-valid) reason [4]. In the same vein, international arbitrators, having to decide on compensation in very similar cases, vary on discrete issues such as the applicable interest rate - with the unsettling result that some monetary awards will double in value in a few years, while others are set to decrease due to negative interest rate [6].

Seen under this light, many institutional legal devices can be understood as a manner to control this subjectivity and corral human legal opinions towards a "right" outcome: for instance, most legal systems recognise an adversarial principle, which allows both parties to debate a legal point, on the assumptions that parties are incentivised to marshal the "best" legal arguments in their favour, nudging the dispute's resolution towards the legally-mandated outcome. Yet, that assumption is not always met, as parties sometimes have other incentives: for instance, sophisticated parties may deliberately initiate losing cases to set a precedent helpful down the line [2]. Meanwhile, the various appellate stages in hierarchical legal systems are also supposed to correct legal deviations and impose a single answer. Yet, this too finds limitations, notably in the typical problem that one stage is final, and *quis custodiet ipsos custodes*? Besides, not every case can be appealed to the final stage, and an outcome might depend on the (often, random) composition of the appellate bodies.

The Indeterminacy of the Law. The variance in legal decision-making is also a function of the indeterminacy of the underlying norms. Laws, by their nature, cannot dictate outcomes for every conceivable situation, which is why their application and enforcement is mostly delegated to systems (e.g., police, courts, and tribunals) able to accommodate new and unexpected circumstances. The "open texture" of the law proceeds from its polysemous language [8], leading to areas of vagueness where judicial discretion plays a pivotal role.

This ambiguity allows for flexibility, but also introduces variability in how laws are interpreted and applied. Indeed, as judges fill gaps in the legal framework by appealing to principles meant to provide systemic coherence, they run the risk of injecting variability into legal outcomes. Given the non-linear dynamics and feedback loops of legal systems (as precedents go on to influence later outcomes), it suffices that individuals differ even slightly as to what "coherence" entails for the entire system to reach a state of fractal inconsistencies.

Further, the hiatus between the enactment of a norm and its application may see a change in the circumstances that motivated the law in the first place, or the tenets of its application might have evolved in such a manner than a strict interpretation becomes untenable. In other words, norms does not exist in a vacuum, and may have to evolve in response to shifting societal norms and values. Judicial decisions often acquire a landmark character when they reinterpret longstanding legal principles in light of contemporary societal contexts. The dynamic nature of societal values therefore contributes to the indeterminacy of law, necessitating a degree of judicial discretion and interpretation - in other words, of variance.

Variance for the Legal System. While often necessary, the variance introduced by the human element in legal decision-making is frequently seen as an issue to be tackled. At stake are the cornerstone principles of consistency and predictability of justice, key for the legitimacy and credibility of legal systems. To the extent a legal system generates reliance and legitimate expectations in those it governs [11], the frustration of these expectations sounds in arbitrariness. In turn, perceptions of arbitrariness can quickly erode trust in third-party decision-making–regardless of the ground truth of that perception. For instance, the International Court of Justice suffered a deficit of trust in the 70s and 80s, following a set of rulings that have been interpreted as reflecting a conservative approach to decolonisation and self-determination issues, in a context where many new states arose from that decolonisation. This resulted in a much-reduced caseload for the Court, which only picked up pace at the turn of the century.

On the other hand, this variance has systemic advantages, as it serves as a fundamental mechanism for the evolution and adaptation of jurisprudence, ensuring that legal principles remain responsive to the complexities of human society, unprecedented challenges are addressed, and oversights in the legal framework are corrected [10]. Judicial discretion allows for the nuanced application of laws to a diverse array of cases, acknowledging that the rigid application of a rule may not always lead to just outcomes - hence the role of "equity" in various legal domains, a concept elaborated in clear contra-distinction with "black letter" law.

Put another way, variance in judicial decision-making functions as an information-collection device, that propagates through the system signals about the potential lack of fit between norms and the underlying circumstances. These signals may result in "jurisprudential splits" across different courts or judicial levels, calling for a resolution, either judicial (e.g., the US Supreme Court takes up cases where the lower appeal courts are divided) or legislative. Knowing this, the craft of jurists at every stage includes challenging not only the application of a norm, but also, sometimes, the norm itself (e.g., through a declaration of unconstitutionality). In answer, judges introduce variance, either through clear break with the past (when a solution is overturned), or where they add to the exceptions to a legal concept, generating complexity that might later trip any reasoning by analogy.

The resulting tension between "bad" (arbitrary, inconsistent) and "good" (flexible, pertinent) variance permeates the entire legal system. Contrasted decisions may enrich (and/or complicate) case law, contributing to the depth and breadth (or inconsistency) of legal precedents. As judges encounter unique cases, their varied interpretations and rulings weave a richer tapestry of jurisprudence, offering a more comprehensive legal framework for addressing future disputes. Yet, and of course, this tapestry of jurisprudence then offer more ways and avenues for jurists to introduce ever-greater variance in the system: deviations from the rule in one case becomes the argument for further deviations in other cases–again, based on the idea that likes should be treated alike. This has contributed to the long-standing view that the craft of lawyers is one of chicanery and self-serving subtlety.

In other words, variance is key to understand many aspects of a legal/judicial system, and shows up as a practical avenue to solve the tension between the need for legal adaptability and the demand for consistency.

3 Variance in Machine Learning

Algorithmic Determinism. Traditional algorithms operate on a foundation of deterministic logic, where specific inputs lead to predictable, unchanging outputs. These algorithms are governed by a set of predefined rules and procedures that dictate their operation, ensuring a high degree of reliability and consistency in their outcomes.

The deterministic nature of such algorithms makes them well-suited for tasks with clear, well-defined parameters and objectives, where the desired outcome is known and can be directly programmed into the algorithm's logic. On the other hand, this has proven to be a limit to the deployment of such traditional algorithms in the legal domain. As a matter of output, the wide array of solutions and remedies embraced by judicial discretion has represented a hurdle for rule-based algorithms.

More importantly, and as noted above, legal language, just as language in general, has a polysemous nature, making it difficult to reduce it to the inputs required of a machine learning algorithm. For instance, the term "consideration" in contract law can denote something significantly different from its common usage, and its legal interpretation can vary based on jurisdictional nuances and case-specific contexts. While a process of translation is therefore required, the specifics of this process generate many difficulties, especially in terms of what losses of subtlety and nuance are tolerable for the model to have any concrete application.

These difficulties are highlighted by the limits of the Rules as Code and "computable law" approaches, which, when hyped as a silver bullet to reduce legal complexity and automate legal reasoning, have typically fallen short in capturing the interpretative flexibility inherent in legal practice.

Machine Learning Flexibility. In contrast to the rigid structure of traditional algorithms, machine learning introduces a level of adaptability and learning capacity that allows models to adjust and improve based on the data they are exposed to. Neural networks, a cornerstone of modern machine learning, exemplify this flexibility through their ability to approximate complex functions and capture patterns in data that are not readily apparent or easily programmable.

The introduction of variance and randomness in the training of machine learning processes, such as through the initialization of weights, the selection of samples, or the random dropout of neurons during training, has proven beneficial in improving model training and convergence [13]. The key method of Stochastic Gradient Descent (SGD) provides a prime example, as it relies on the random selection of samples for computing the gradient of the loss function, which helps in escaping local minima and exploring the solution space more effectively. As such, in many modern approaches, randomness and variance are not merely a byproduct but a fundamental aspect that enables models to avoid being trapped in sub-optimal configurations.

Variance has also found a place at the level of outputs, for instance through the use of "temperature" in large language models. Adjusting the temperature parameter affects the randomness of the model's predictions, allowing for a tuneable balance between creativity and accuracy/consistency. Higher temperatures can yield more novel and varied outputs, whereas lower temperatures produce more deterministic, expected results.

Variance for Machine Learning. However, the introduction of stochastic elements and the complexity of machine learning algorithms bring forth challenges, particularly regarding predictability and transparency. The randomness inherent in SGD can lead to fluctuations in the learning path, potentially impacting the stability and convergence speed of the training process. Hence the development of variance-reduced methods to balance the exploration benefits of stochasticity with the need for stable, predictable, and efficient training processes [14]. Some further methods try to achieve the best of both worlds, in managing the tension between variance and consistency (i.e., regularisation) [9].

Likewise, variance in deployment has often been considered an issue - for instance, arising from underspecification - that calls for dedicated methods to mitigate it. And while such variance can be beneficial for certain applications, it can also complicate tasks that require consistent and replicable results. For instance, in medical diagnostics, varying predictions from an AI model can complicate clinical decision-making processes, where consistent and accurate diagnoses are critical. Here as well, variance can be mitigated through further methods, for instance by combining the ensemble of the predictions of multiple models, so as to average out individual variances.

Moreover, the "black box" nature of many complex models, such as deep neural networks, complicates efforts to understand and interpret how decisions are made, entailing challenges for accountability and trust, especially in critical applications. "Explainability" of AI has become a lightning rod in the debates about AI and the law, from both sides of the law/tech divide, partly because of these issues of variance and indeterminacy [3].

4 The Role of Automated Variance in Legal Decision-Making

The preceding sections have established that variance, be it in the legal or technical domain, engender similar issues. In both cases, the stochasticity that contributes to a system's flexibility and adaptability can become a liability, necessitating mechanisms to ensure that outputs remain within acceptable bounds of consistency.

Invariance and Its Issues. While justice has so far been dispensed mostly by humans (sometimes, professing to act on behalf of gods), those are not necessary: what matters is that the outcomes are perceived as fair and sound, supplemented (if required) by reasons that just need to be persuasive enough. Even if it may take time, there is thus no principled ground why AI systems should not eventually assist, if not replace judges, to the extent they become sufficiently cost-effective [7].

This cost-effectiveness is favourable to the AI side for one particular reason: by contrast with human judges, and assuming that the AI system has been competently trained and deployed [16], one of the key benefits of AI systems is precisely their capacity to reduce variance and noise in decision-making–or, to come back to the critical principle highlighted above, to ensure that likes are treated alike. Moreover, since automated legal systems can be expected to also be cost-effective in terms of pure monetary costs, they promise a greater and more comprehensive scope of enforcement, decreasing the rate of legal evasion, and once again contributing to the fundamental notion of equality before the law.

Yet, this strength might also be a flaw in some circumstances: much has already been made of the potential for AI systems to perpetuate, or even exacerbate, existing biases–through unbalanced training data or flawed algorithmic assumptions. All told, there could be circumstances where arbitrary justice might be preferable to a consistently unfair AI system [10].

On top of this, some laws are not always expected to be "perfectly" enforced - some norms are constantly broken (e.g., jaywalking), others exist more to convey a message than for enforcement purposes, and yet others have been adopted with expectations that clemency and leniency, or even empathy, would mitigate their application. Legal norms also routinely preserve a margin of discretion for decision-makers. Needless to say, there are challenges to replicate these sources of variance in the context of an automated AI system [5]. Some recent experiments have laid bare that AI systems, when deployed to assist judicial decision-making, are routinely ignored for failing to take into account the full dimension of a legal case [15]. Moreover, and as noted earlier, judicial systems are also geared towards allowing (if not encouraging) legal subjects to *request* variance, by contesting the validity of a norm itself, or by claiming that it should yield in front of another norm–features that are also challenging to replicate in automated decision-making.

Besides, and as seen above, variance has a role to play in a legal system, begging the question of whether legal algorithms should integrate that dimension, and how.

The Pitfalls of Automated Variance. The introduction of AI with variance into the legal system raises several technological and legal dilemmas.

Key among these is the challenge of accountability, i.e., of determining responsibility for AI-driven decisions, especially when outcomes are unpredictable or when the decision-making process is opaque. The "black box" nature of many AI systems complicates efforts to trace the logic behind specific decisions, raising concerns about transparency and the ability to challenge AI-generated outcomes in legal contexts. And all the more so with respect to automated variance, as any potential "victim" of such variance could legitimately protest that their fate should not depend on an algorithmic, probabilistic decision to deviate deliberately baked in the system by its designers. In other words, while under a veil of ignorance everyone could rationally agree on automated variance, in reality no one would accept to be prejudiced by it.

And to the extent that variance is helpful to help the law progress, this begs the question as to *when* variance is needed, or when a series of consistent decisions should be amended - what is known in jurisprudential theory as the tipping point problem [11]. In turn, this raises questions as to various types of norms or precedents that could/should be departed with, and with what ease, an issue that touches upon greater considerations of politics or morals. Indeed, different aspects of variance may require different answers: variance generated by cases of first impression, or where the law is obscure/complex/indeterminate, may not be the same or equally-desired as variance introduced as a result of political choices (i.e., when judges appointed as the result of a political process opt to overturn precedents).

These issues partly stem from the distinct sources of variance in humans and machines. Human variability is deeply rooted in the experiential, ethical, and contextual considerations of human judges, whereas AI variability is largely a function of data, algorithmic structure, and the stochastic processes inherent in machine learning. Asking the latter to conform with the former, for instance by seeking a "conservative" or "liberal" form of variance, is fraught with legitimacy concerns. In fact, and fundamentally, it is unclear whether variance can even be deliberate or whether it *just has to happen*, just like one cannot force oneself to fall in love, or decide to have adventures.

Indeed, it may be that variance in legal decision-making is one of those things that survive only because they are protected by a myth that no one should try to probe. Stripping away the veneer to reveal the underlying assumptions of a legal system - that likes cases are resolved alike - may destabilize the very foundations of that system. The legal domain operates effectively because of a collective faith in its functionality and necessity, a delicate balance maintained by the shared conviction of its stakeholders. Translating the nuanced, often tacit principles of law–such as the need for variance, however unfair to the individual case decided differently–into the explicit, rigid codifications required by computational systems might not only expose, but also disrupt, this precarious equilibrium, challenging the implicit trust that sustains the legal system's authority and integrity.

Principles of Automated Variance in Legal Decision-Making. As such, the integration of AI in legal decision-making will necessitate a careful consideration of the dual need for consistency and variability in judicial decisions. Put otherwise: legal AI systems must balance the innovation and adaptability offered by algorithmic variability with the foundational legal principle that similar cases should yield similar outcomes. Achieving this balance requires a nuanced understanding of the roles that both humans and machines play in the legal ecosystem.

The following principles would be beneficial to that integration:

- To the extent that it is possible to distinguish between bad variance (or "arbitrariness") and good variance (e.g., evolution of the law), the judicial system should dedicate a procedure to rule on that distinction in appropriate cases, mostly leaving that task to humans.
- Variance would be more adequate in circumstances that evidence a large feeling or injustice, or where legal subjects do not rely strongly on the law (or expect it to change soon). This could require feeding AI systems with further data (e.g., appeal numbers, social sentiment) to probe those circumstances, as well as feedback mechanisms for the system to know when and to what extent outcomes have varied.
- To ensure greater legitimacy, most automated variance should be of the non-openly-politicised type, leaving the legislative process as the primary instrument for legal changes induced by the political system, in line with the principle of separation of powers.
- To the extent variance is deliberately introduced in the algorithm, the features of that variance (e.g., in terms of probability or conditions) should not be disclosed, failing which litigants would seek to game the system. On the other hand, to ensure public engagement and trust, it appears difficult to hide the fact that an AI system has been designed to accommodate some deliberate variance.
- In any event, a further decision should be made as to whether a result obtained through automated variance in individual case should or should not affect that particular case - an issue familiar to judges, used to decide if their reasoning should operate *ex tunc* or *ex nunc*. That issue, too, could be left to human judges.

Following these principles will require institutional and cultural changes to the common approaches to the law, which should treat variance as a legal object worthy of legal analysis in itself–and not simply something that happens despite ourselves, to be managed if at all while denying its existence. It goes without saying, of course, that any decisions about variance are bound to be inconsistent as well, raising questions as to how the legal system should deal with the variance of the sample variance.

References

1. Shapiro, M.: Courts - A Comparative and Political Analysis. The University of Chicago Press, Chicago (1981)
2. Daku, M., Pelc, K.J.: Who holds influence over WTO jurisprudence? J. Int. Econ. Law **20**, 233–255 (2017)
3. Bennetot, A., et al.: A practical guide on explainable AI techniques applied on biomedical use case applications. Electronic copy. https://arxiv.org/abs/2111.14260
4. Raman, V., Vera, C., Manna, C.J.: Bias, consistency, and partisanship in U.S. asylum cases: a machine learning analysis of extraneous factors in immigration court decisions (2022). https://doi.org/10.1145/3551624.3555288
5. Hartzog, W., Conti, G., Nelson, J., Shay, L.A.: Inefficiently automated law enforcement. Mich. State Law Rev. 1763–1796 (2015)
6. Charlotin, D., Greenwood, L., Diaz-Cordova, L.: Noises off: towards greater consistency in international arbitration awards. J. Intl. Arbitration **392**, 213–232 (2022)
7. Volokh, E.: Chief justice robots. Duke Law J. **68**, 1135–92 (2019)
8. Bix, B.: Law, Language, and Legal Determinacy. Clarendon Press, Oxford (1981)
9. Zhu, J., Shwartz-Ziv, R., Chen, Y., LeCun, Y.: Variance-covariance regularization improves representation learning. arXiv preprint arXiv:2306.13292 (2023)
10. Custers, B.: The right to break the law? Perfect enforcement of the law using technology impedes the development of legal systems. Ethics Inf. Technol. **25** (2023)
11. Levin, H.Y.: A reliance approach to precedent. Ga. L. Rev. **47**, 1035 (2012)
12. Morin-Martel, A.: Machine learning in bail decisions and judges' trustworthiness. AI Soc. **39**, 2033–2044 (2024)
13. Glorot, X., Bengiot, Y.: Understanding the difficulty of training deep feedforward neural networks. In: AISTATS, JMLR Proceedings, vol. 9, pp. 249–256 (2010)
14. Gower, R. M., Schmidt, M., Bach, F., Richtárik, P.: Variance-reduced methods for machine learning. In: Proc. IEEE **108**(11), 1968–1983 (2020)
15. Stevenson, M. T., Doleac, J. L.: Algorithmic risk assessment in the hands of humans. Electronic copy. https://ssrn.com/abstract=3489440
16. Greene, T., Shmueli, G., Fell, J., Lin, C.-F., Liu, H.-W.: Forks over knives: predictive inconsistency in criminal justice algorithmic risk assessment tools. arXiv preprint arXiv:2012.00289 (2020). https://doi.org/10.48550/arXiv.2012.00289
17. Edge, R.: The necessary evolution of privacy program automation. OneTrust (2022). https://www.onetrust.com/blog/the-necessary-evolution-of-privacy-program-automation/

Evaluating AI for Law: Bridging the Gap with Open-Source Solutions

Rohan Bhambhoria[1,2], Samuel Dahan[1,2,3](✉), Jonathan Li[2], and Xiaodan Zhu[1,2]

[1] Queen's University, Kingston, ON K7L3N6, Canada
{r.bhambhoria,xiaodan.zhu}@queensu.ca
[2] Ingenuity Labs, Ontario, Canada
{samuel.dahan,jxl}@queensu.ca
[3] Cornell University, Ithaca, USA

Abstract. This study evaluates the performance of general-purpose AI, like ChatGPT, in legal question-answering tasks, highlighting significant risks to legal professionals and clients. It suggests leveraging foundational models enhanced by domain-specific knowledge to overcome these issues. The paper advocates for creating open-source legal AI systems to improve accuracy, transparency, and narrative diversity, addressing general AI's shortcomings in legal contexts.

Keywords: Law · Open-Source · Large Language Models

1 Introduction

In recent times, the rise of Large Language Models (LLMs) has become prominent, especially with the unprecedented growth of ChatGPT, marking it as the fastest-expanding consumer application to date. LLMs have shown extensive utility in tasks related to productivity and in systems designed for low-stakes decision-making, such as composing emails. However, its application in high-stakes decision-making areas, including contract drafting or medical diagnostics, is met with cautious adaptation due to concerns about its large-scale deployment.

We believe that Artificial Intelligence-powered legal advice, or "legal AI," can improve access to justice and contribute more broadly to the practice of law, increasing the percentage of adequately-represented litigants and driving down legal fees and the cost of legal research [31]. Research has shown that legal AI can help to assist self-represented litigants with tasks such as determining the validity of a claim, online dispute resolution and court filing [6,21]. However, AI remains plagued with limitations, including the phenomenon of "hallucination" and the potential for biased advice [9]; and there is anecdotal evidence of reliance —even over reliance [36], on the use of generative AI tools for legal advice. Alarmingly, this is true among both self-represented litigants and legal practitioners themselves [9].

© The Author(s), under exclusive license to Springer Nature Switzerland AG 2026
D. Restrepo Amariles and K. Satoh (Eds.): *Compliance for Artificial Intelligence Systems*, LNAI 14377, pp. 59–74, 2026.
https://doi.org/10.1007/978-3-032-12795-2_5

The problem is further exacerbated by the proliferation of so-called AI applications specialised for law, many of which are built on top of general-purpose systems such as GPT-4.[1] These applications, misleadingly presented as specialized legal tools, mask the underlying limitations of the technology. These systems, which are closed, raise transparency and accessibility concerns; conflict with the movement towards open science; and hinder understanding of AI knowledge [20]. Furthermore, these technologies are accessible primarily by large firms, thus offering limited benefit to broader legal communities and doing nothing to improve access to justice.

Finally, current regulations, such as the EU AI Act and Canada's AIDA (Artificial Intelligence and Data Act), do not yet provide solid benchmarks for addressing these issues. Policymakers need to debate the accessibility, quality, impact, and design of legal AI in order to produce industry standards for its creation and use. Anything less not only hinders access to justice, but risks hurting the very people who stand to gain the most from its development.

We propose two solutions to address the identified challenges: (i) revising benchmarks and protocols to evaluating legal AI's performance capabilities and limitations in real-world settings, and (ii) based on performance findings, creating a domain-specific, open-source language model interface that allows for diverse feedback collection.

Acknowledging the current AI regulations' inadequacies in managing generative AI's risks in legal contexts, we advocate for a sector-specific approach to define reliable legal AI systems. This includes developing benchmarks specifically tailored to legal challenges, focusing on legal misinformation, transparency, and diversity in narrative representation. Utilizing computational benchmarking, we aim to develop evaluation metrics centered on Bias Risk, Fact-Checking, Legal Reasoning Ability, and Narrative Construction Diversity for application in question-answering tasks.

Drawing from performance insights, we explore legal AI solutions that may show significant improvement over general-purpose AI. Specifically, we highlight the potential of an open-source approach through OpenJustice.ai—a platform that encourages collaborative and crowdsourced efforts to design and test custom AI solutions for legal professionals and aid centers. This approach promotes a transparent and inclusive method of AI development, allowing diverse perspectives and expertise to contribute to more ethical and robust AI systems.

An essential aspect of this domain-specific solution is the emphasis on data curation. The quality of data used to train these models is crucial for their reliability and effectiveness [34]. Proper data curation entails not only gathering extensive and diverse datasets but also ensuring the data is representative, unbiased, and pertinent to the specific legal applications.

---

[1] https://www.thomsonreuters.com/en/press-releases/2024/april/thomson-reuters-announces-expanded-vision-to-provide-genai-assistant-for-every-professional-it-serves.html.

2 Background: AI Is Not Yet Ready for Law

Recent studies indicate a concerning trend in artificial intelligence: the as-yet-unexplained "drifting" phenomenon, characterized by significant fluctuations in AI's capabilities [38]. For example, in one study, an AI system's accuracy rate in solving basic math problems dropped from 98% to 2% in the space of months. Certainly in the legal context, evidence has shown that despite AI's capacity to perform some legal tasks —even passing the bar exam [4] —the technology has not yet fully matured. Generative AI is prone to "hallucinating" inaccurate responses with confidence, offering biased advice and erroneous citations [8]. A further problem is that LLMs tend to reflect a mainstream worldview. When they are a primary source of AI training data, feedback loops are created wherein AI-generated texts are reincorporated into the web, creating "AI echo chambers" [3].

1. Hallucinations, and Confident Regurgitation. Recent studies have demonstrated that generative AI is capable of executing a variety of legal tasks and has even successfully passed the bar examination [4]. However, the technology still has significant limitations. A well-documented issue with generative AI architectures is their tendency to produce *hallucinated* responses [37]. These responses are characterized by high confidence levels in presenting incorrect information, including the fabrication of facts, citations, and details. Generalized LLMs such as ChatGPT operate by predicting a sequence of words that logically follows an initial user-provided input. This process incorporates an element of creativity, wherein the model randomly selects elements of a sentence from a set of probable responses. This method, while innovative, also contributes to the challenge of ensuring accuracy and reliability in the generated content, particularly in contexts that demand high precision, like legal tasks.

In essence, AI systems primarily operate on statistical principles and thus possess limited comprehension capabilities, particularly in specialized domains such as law. The generative models currently in use demonstrate a notable deficiency in capturing the semantic subtleties inherent in legal terminology. This limitation is exemplified by the varying interpretations of the same legal term across different jurisdictions. For instance, the term *layoff* is interpreted as *suspension* in Canada, whereas it denotes *termination* in the United States. A more pressing concern is the deceptive proficiency of generative AI systems in understanding legal concepts. Despite appearances, these systems often lack the capability for counterfactual legal reasoning or the classification of different modes of legal reasoning. This shortfall highlights the gap between the apparent and actual capabilities of AI in complex, context-dependent fields such as law [5].

This limitation may be inconsequential for tasks that are statistical in nature, such as the retrieval of legal precedents or the application of straightforward rules to facts. However, it presents a significant challenge for more complex legal reasoning tasks, which require a multidimensional approach and an in-depth understanding of legal issues. Beyond the problem of *hallucinations* or the generation of inaccurate content, there are also concerns regarding biased analyses. This is a well-documented issue in the application of predictive AI in legal contexts, as referenced in [6] and [7]. For instance, ChatGPT, like many AI systems, has been shown to exhibit biases that are commonly observed in human reasoning. These include conjunction bias, probability weighting, overconfidence, framing effects, anticipated regret, reference dependence, and confirmation bias, as detailed in [8]. Such biases can significantly affect the objectivity and reliability of AI-generated legal analyses, underscoring the need for cautious application and rigorous evaluation of these technologies in legal settings.

2. Lack of Diversity in Generated Responses. The implications of employing LLMs in the realm of computational linguistics are not limited to issues of inaccuracies or the dissemination of misinformation in legal contexts. A significant concern arises even when generative AI systems like LLMs provide accurate information. These concerns stem from the inherent tendency of general-purpose LLMs to replicate dominant worldviews. If LLMs become a prevalent source of information, there is a potential for creating feedback loops. In such scenarios, the text generated by LLMs could re-enter the digital ecosystem, effectively becoming part of the training dataset for subsequent generations of text-generating models. This could lead to the development of *AI echo chambers*, as articulated in [3]. Such chambers could substantially limit the diversity of thought, posing a risk to the breadth of intellectual discourse and possibly affecting the development of AI systems in ways that could hinder cultural diversity, narrative plurality, and the dynamism of democratic discourse.

3. Linear Reasoning. In the development and application of LLMs for legal domains, several critical issues emerge. Unlike fields with clear, mathematical solutions, law encompasses a spectrum of acceptable answers and allows for considerable discretion. This characteristic renders the use of LLMs in legal contexts not merely as tools for information retrieval, but as systems that inherently shape the representation of legal information. The first concern with such LLMs is the presumption that legal issues are algorithmic, necessitating straightforward solutions. This assumption contradicts the reality of legal practice, where different lawyers and judges often propose divergent solutions to identical legal scenarios, as evidenced in sources [6,21,22]. A common lawyer's response, *it depends*, highlights this variability.

4. Lack of Temporal Dimension in Legal Applications. LLMs often operate on the assumption that the facts and contexts of future legal cases will mirror those of the past, disregarding the dynamic nature of social contexts that continuously introduce new facts and legal challenges. This approach risks stagnating the legal field, potentially leading to the ossification and de-norming of law.

5. Static Training Databases. A further complication arises from the opaqueness of generative AI systems like LLMs, which often cannot cite their information sources. This is particularly problematic in legal practice, where the substantiation of arguments with appropriate legal citations is crucial. The inability of LLMs to reliably cite sources, and their tendency to generate fictitious case law or legislation poses significant risks. While models like GPT-4 have shown capabilities to reference relevant statutes and legal authorities, they continue to exhibit limitations in generating accurate connections and in incorporating new legal developments, given their training on a static dataset representing a snapshot of the internet at a particular time.

Yet, despite these sizable concerns, there is little empirical data about AI performance in legal context. Most knowledge stems from GPT-4's varied performance on legal exams [10–12] and discrete questions [13,14], alongside theoretical discussions on AI's ethical use [15] and its impact on legal skills and firm competitiveness [16]. Research reveals GPT-4's inconsistent exam results and its challenges in issue identification and rule application, noting its potential to assist lower-performing students without benefiting top achievers [17]. Limited evidence exists outside exams, with some studies highlighting AI's potential in legal reasoning and others cautioning against overreliance due to AI's hallucinations and misinterpretations.

In fact LegalBench [33] is a collaborative project designed to benchmark the legal reasoning capabilities of LLMs using the IRAC framework. Its goal is to assess how well current AI models can support and augment legal reasoning, particularly in administrative and transactional settings, without aiming to replace legal professionals. In contrast, our project diverges by focusing on applying AI to practical, real-world legal tasks comprising of hypotheticals and factual questions, concerning self-represented litigants through a domain-specific, open-source platform. We aim to directly evaluate AI's effectiveness in performing tasks that mirror the day-to-day work of legal professionals, moving beyond theoretical benchmarks to assess practical utility and integration into legal workflows.

Contrastingly, recent work investigates AI's capabilities in contract review, a narrowly defined task where AI has been shown to excel, even outperforming lawyers in previous studies [18,19]. This focus contrasts with our project, which extends beyond document analysis to cover a broader range of practical legal tasks through a domain-specific, open-source platform, aiming to assess AI's utility in a wider legal context.

Finally, recent work by Choi et al., presents meaningful insights into how AI may augment the performance of some lawyers, particularly the lower-performing ones. However, it also primarily focuses on tasks that are relatively easier for LLMs, such as drafting legal documents and answering hypothetical questions with provided materials. Our project aims to bridge these gaps by providing a more detailed and nuanced examination of AI's capabilities and deficiencies in a broader range of legal tasks, moving beyond the realms explored by the aforementioned studies. This endeavor not only highlights AI's current limitations in legal practice but also advocates for a targeted approach towards developing domain-specific, open-source legal AI solutions to address these challenges effectively.

Our preliminary study aims to advance the literature on AI benchmarking focusing on evaluating GPT-4's assistance in practical lawyering [17] tasks - especially Question-Answer, aiming to advance the understanding of AI's qualitative impacts in law.

3 Datasets and Statistics

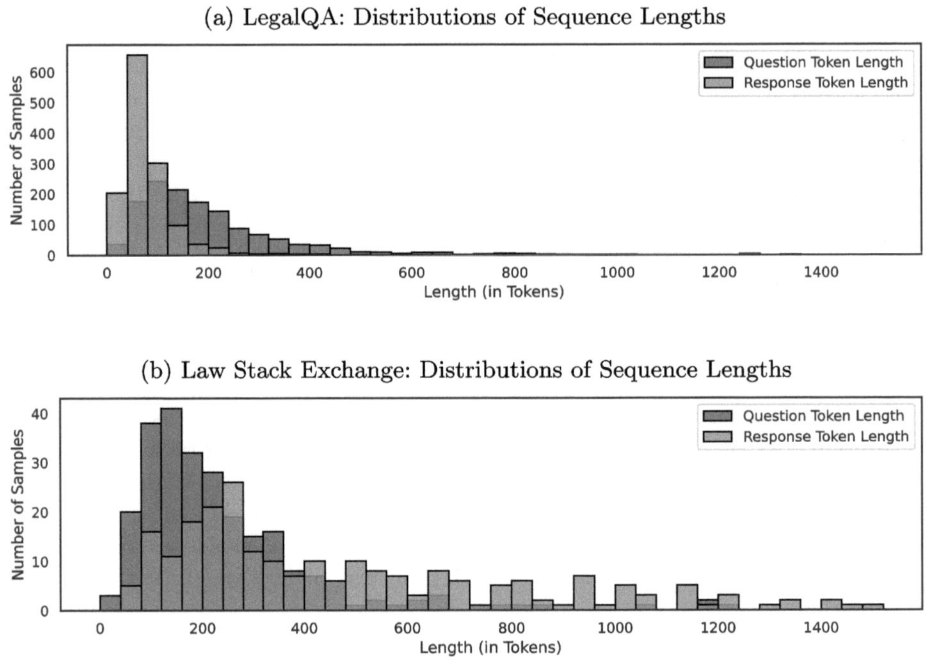

Fig. 1. Distribution of sequence lengths for LegalQA and Law Stack Exchange. We measure the length in tokens (with byte-pair encoding) and combine the train and test sets.

In this work, we curate a legal QA benchmark to reflect real-world scenarios. Existing legal benchmarks, such as LegalBench [33], often lack real-world hypothetical and fact-based analysis aspects present in real-world legal challenges. Specifically, *most* LegalBench tasks are classification problems, which fail to evaluate various dimensions desirable for a language model in aiding laypeople with legal tasks.

To this end, we curate LegalQA, a high-quality dataset of over 2000 questions asked by laypeople on real legal questions and answers vetted by legal experts. We ask law students to write expert answers to these questions (process described in more detail in Sect. 3.1). The questions are sourced from an online legal community.[2]

In conjunction with our new dataset, we also source additional legal questions from Law Stack Exchange and collect the 200 most popular questions on the site (to serve as a proxy for questions that people find interesting/challenging to solve). Then, we use the top-voted answer for each question as the expert label.

[2] https://reddit.com/r/legaladvice.

These two datasets, from differing online platforms, address different domains. For example, the longer sequence lengths visible in Fig. 1 reflect differences in data collection methodologies; we encourage our law students to answer the question as concisely as possible (while addressing everything in the question), whereas top stack exchange answers often directly copy a long block quotation to cite their sources clearly, increasing length. Together, these two datasets provide an evaluation of a model's capabilities of addressing a layperson's legal concerns across various settings.

3.1 Annotation Guidelines

We designed a data labelling procedure to build the most robust answers. Following principles described in Sect. 6.2, we ask our human annotators to highlight relevant facts in the legal question, write a concise answer, and provide a link to a reliable source of further reading.

Since our law students are trained under Canadian law, we ask law students to consider questions on U.S. law from a Canadian perspective. If it is impossible to contextualize within a Canadian legal framework (e.g., if the question concerns specific gun laws), then we omit this data. Otherwise, if the question asks about the law that is answerable with Canadian law, then our annotators will treat it under a Canadian context. We consider these laws from a Canadian perspective to maintain annotations that are verifiable by our Canadian legal experts.

Regarding the format of answers, we ask annotators to limit answers to 200–300 characters, and to stay as close to the evidence as possible —this is to mirror a real-world legal environment where making concise and evidence-driven answers is important. Additionally, we ask annotators to avoid using legalese and explain in terms understandable by a general audience (the target audience). We include an example annotation in Table 1.

4 Experimental Setup

To evaluate the landscape of current language models, we run experiments on state-of-the-art closed and open-sourced models. Specifically, we evaluate OpenAI's most recent GPT-4 model, GPT-4-Turbo-1106 (hereinafter called "GPT-4") since it is the state-of-the-art general-purpose language model at the time of writing. For the open-sourced model, we evaluated Mixtral-8x7B,[3] a state-of-the-art mixture of experts chat-aligned language model with 46.7B parameters.

We evaluate the factuality (as opposed to style) of the resulting generations. Since the real-world nature of this benchmark facilitates open-ended responses, it is difficult to evaluate model responses without human feedback. As a proxy for human evaluation, we evaluate the generated answers relative to the expert answer automatically with a language model, based on the opensource automatic

[3] https://mistral.ai/news/mixtral-of-experts/.

Table 1. Example question ("source") and provided answers and citation. The highlighted green portion denotes the relevant facts indicated by the annotator.

Source	... my partner and I have been renting from a deadbeat property management company for the last year. There was a maintenance issue and a flooding issue 2 months after we moved in. We brought to their attention, they gave it a bandaid fix and have been ignoring any contact since (I have records of all of the attempts to contact them). We have called, texted, emailed, and my partner even went to their office to try and speak to someone and basically got blown off by the guy at the front desk who is one of the main agents for this company. Luckily, the issue hasn't caused damage to any of our personal property, but if it goes unfixed will inevitably damage the house itself and become a much bigger issue. Suffice to say, we're not interested in continuing to rent from them. The issue I'm seeking advice on is that we got an email asking if we're interested in renewing (for $50 more a month for another 12 months) and they are requesting we give notice by 3/1 if we intend to vacate. Our lease we signed says we must provide notice by 3/31, not 3/1. It's a difficult time all around to find a new place to rent that fits into our timeline and budget and I want as much time as we can so we don't have to overlap leasing and also to guarantee we can actually find something before our lease is up at the end of April. So my question is: should/can I send an email saying the lease we signed says we don't have to give notice until 3/31 whether or not we'll renew and that they can expect our answer then? Although they can request we give them more advanced notice, contractually, I don't think we're obligated to. Any advice would be greatly appreciated and thanks for taking the time to read this.
Provided answer	In Ontario, in a fixed-term tenancy, you must give at least a 60-day notice before the end of the lease. If not the tenancy continues. If the tenancy agreement does not say what happens after the end of the fixed-term, your lease will continue on a month-to-month basis automatically. A landlord cannot force you to agree to end a tenancy.
Provided citation	https://www.siskinds.com/pet-custody-laws-in-ontario

evaluation repository, OpenAI Evals.[4] As OpenAI Evals were created for general-purpose evaluations, we would like to highlight the need and requirement for improvements in the legal domain. We use GPT-4 for this automatic evaluation, asking it to compare the model-generated answer to the expert answer, and indicating if the answer is a subset of the expert answer, a superset of the expert answer, contains the same details as the expert answer, disagrees with the expert answer, or answers the question in a incomparable way to the expert answer (see Table 2). Then, we ask legal experts to review the model's evaluations to assess their reliability.

[4] https://github.com/openai/evals.

Table 2. Classes used to automatically evaluate the factuality of model generations.

Category	Description
A ($\subset$)	The submitted answer is a subset of the expert answer and is fully consistent with it.
B ($\supset$)	The submitted answer is a superset of the expert answer and is fully consistent with it.
C ($=$)	The submitted answer contains all the same details as the expert answer.
D ($\neq$)	There is a disagreement between the submitted answer and the expert answer.
E ($\stackrel{?}{\approx}$)	It is not possible to compare the answers directly for factuality because the submitted answer addresses the question differently from the expert answer.

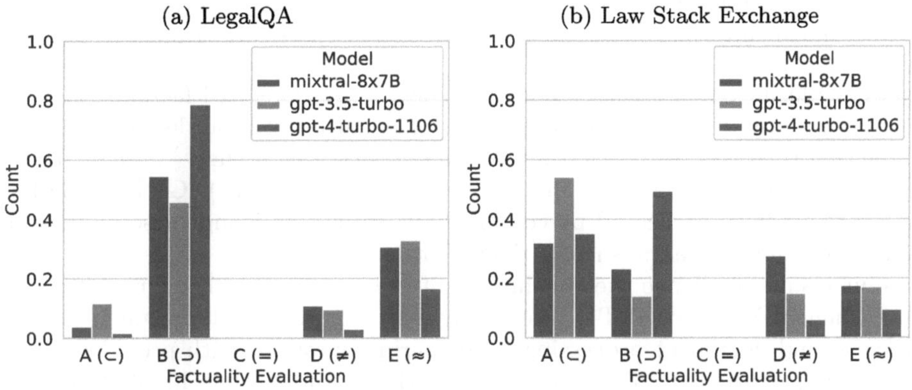

Fig. 2. Automatic evaluation results for (a) LegalQA and (b) Law Stack Exchange. Experimental setting described in Sect. 3.1.

Our experiments reveal two insights. First, they evaluate various models in legal question answering. Second, they shed light on the capabilities of language models to be used for evaluation—something that is now done regularly in the general domain but underexplored in the legal domain.

5 Results and Discussion

In this section we conduct experiments showcasing the ability of LLMs in a practical legal question-answering task. Different from benchmarks [33], our task reflects hypotheticals and factual questions which concern self-represented litigants. Benchmark tasks were created from the perspective of lawyers, whereas laypersons would ask questions with a similar distribution to our dataset.

Apparent in Fig. 2, the state-of-the-art language model GPT-4 seems to perform relatively well on the LegalQA task, with under 5% of examples containing factually incorrect responses. However, we observe that Mixtral 8x7B, a state-of-the-art open language model, falls significantly behind.

Additionally, we hypothesize that a LLM does not evaluate legal texts in the same way as a skilled human lawyer, so we ask law students to evaluate some predictions. The comments as a result of these qualitative observations are shown in Table 3. In general, we observe two phenomena that suggest that, despite the seemingly strong performance of GPT-4, there is still room for improvement:

- **Lack of Citations.** When building a language model; the lack of credible citations given by models like GPT-4 stood out to our annotators —with an open model, it is easier to augment these models with tools, facilitating more trust in the form of citations.
- **Long Winded Answers.** Our annotators found answers written by humans to be more "to the point" and "direct", whereas GPT-4 often provides details that are not related to the legal question. For the examples evaluated, GPT-4 fails to capture the concise answers that legal experts are trained to write.

In the legal domain, these concerns—lack of citations and lack of concision —are especially important due the high-stakes nature of legal decision-making. Given that the tasks tested—LegalQA and Law Stack Exchange—were relatively simple benchmarks (but still ahead of existing benchmarks), GPT-4's performance raises flags, indicated by comments in Table 3 on using these models for even more complex tasks, such as document analysis.

Our results challenge the conclusions of previous studies insofar as it shows that when LLMs, like GPT-4, are subjected to more complex legal reasoning tasks beyond document processing or answering questions with provided material, their performance diminishes. Unlike these studies that highlighted AI's efficiency in relatively straightforward tasks, our experiments reveal limitations in AI's ability to match the nuanced understanding and precise reasoning of human lawyers. Particularly, our findings underscore the issues of inadequate citations and verbosity in AI-generated responses, highlighting the necessity for domain-specific enhancements to meet the rigorous demands of legal practice.

6 A Framework for Legal AI

6.1 The State of Legal AI

Our results suggest that legal industry needs domain-specific solutions. Such systems should be able to handle complex legal reasoning and nuance: after all, in the legal sphere, questions often do not have a single "right answer", but rather a range of acceptable answers. However, the past few years have seen an explosion of so-called generative AIs for law, many of which are actually general-purpose AIs hidden beneath legal-interface veneers. These systems obscure their underlying limitations, despite being presented as specialized tools.

Unfortunately, consensus on the essential criteria for developing legal AI has not yet been reached. There are three primary strategies being considered.

Table 3. Feedback from law students on the automatic evaluations given by GPT-4.

Comments
I prefer the human answer in this particular circumstance. I thought the human answer was more direct an answering the question. It seemed as GPT-4 was providing plenty of details that were not necessarily relevant to overall answer to the question. The human answer also had at least some citations vs GPT-4. Neither opinion really provides much of an analysis of the circumstances.
I prefer the human version. I think the GPT-4 answer is better written, but the human response provides an important citation and answers the question very directly. GPT-4 does not provide the same important citation.
In this case, the specific example given by the human is perfect. It answers the question directly and shows the principles in play by example. GPT-4, while referring more to the example, is quite vague and long-winded in summarising that robbing a bank is stealing.
Human response is far more to the point and interesting. The GPT-4 answer starts by explaining the difference between crimes and civil wrongs without explaining why that's relevant from the start. It could have gone directly into addressing the employer/employer theft concept, while integrating those ideas in. That is more so what the human response offered. The human also gave interesting context and history by mentioning how in certain jurisdictions debt merited imprisonment, or Australia considers wage theft a crime. It gives far more food for thought and is more of what the user was looking for. GPT-4 refers to labour law, but as it doesn't dive in with specifics, its quite vague and bland on the historical aspect.
Both specify there is no policy to prioritise the President of the US in organ transplantation. The human answer provides links to pages informing on the frameworks and mechanisms of organ transplantation. The GPT-4 answer considers the hypothetical case a little but remains vague.
The human answer is superior as it directly references the relevant laws and rules, providing a more precise and targeted response. In contrast, GPT's answer appears somewhat vague, lacking explicit mention of the applicable rules, which could compromise the clarity and specificity of the information provided.

One possibility (Option 1) is to develop a purpose-built, law-specific generative AI model from the ground up. To our knowledge, no such initiative has yet been undertaken in law. It has been undertaken in finance with BloombergGPT [39]; but data on its short- and long-term performance is limited, and recent evidence shows that finance-customized BloombergGPT does not outperform generic GPT4 [40]. To our knowledge, no such initiative has been undertaken in law, likely due to the cost. Furthermore, there is still limited data on short- and long-term performance, and recent evidence shows that BloombergGPT does not perform better than GPT4, a generic model (Li et al. 2023). A more economical choice (Option 2) involves fine-tuning an existing LLM, such as GPT or LLAMA, for legal applications. Early findings indicate that this could be an adequate short-term solution for some legal tasks [33]. Finally, a third option (Option 3) entails training a Small Language Model (SLM) from scratch. Research shows that small-language models, such as Orca 2, can exhibit strong reasoning abilities and outperform larger models by learning from detailed explanation traces [41].

Irrespective of the selected approach, the essential requirement across all solutions requires expertise in both law and computer science. In fact, computational law expertise is vital for constructing, evaluating, and refining legal AI systems. Engaging with professionals possessing this dual expertise is crucial, as they can provide nuanced and informed feedback essential for the continuous improvement of these systems.

However, building an effective legal AI tool extends beyond just expert involvement. Traditional approaches, such as creating closed-system AI platforms accessible only to law firms or those operating on restricted databases, are insufficient [35]. Such approaches, exemplified by platforms like Harvey[5] and LexisNexis's Lexis Plus,[6] fall short in addressing the complexities highlighted in Sect. 2. The limitations of these closed systems, primarily their lack of broad user engagement, can lead to stagnation, failing to adapt to the evolving legal landscape.

6.2 OpenJustice: A Recipe for Building a Crowdsourced Legal Language Model

To overcome these limitations, we propose the development of an open-access legal AI model. Launched in March 2023 by the Conflict Analytics Lab, OpenJustice entered development in January 2021 and operates as a natural-language processing interface, including question-answering, document analysis, and citation retrieval. The system has three layers of data. The first is a core open-source component trained on curated legal data, encompassing thousands of annotated question-answer pairs and case law from the US, Canada, France, and the EU. The second layer relies on crowdsourced human feedback, with OpenJustice handling approximately a few thousands requests per week. Finally, the third layer uses proprietary data from partners to create custom models.

Note that we are experimenting with LLM-fine tuning (Option 2) and training Small Language Models (Option 3). These models are accessible to a wider range of partners, such as law schools, aligning with goals like improving access to justice and legal education. More importantly, this open-access approach can significantly enhance the quality and effectiveness of the AI system. It addresses key issues such as the prevention of AI hallucinations, ensuring factual accuracy, promoting diversity of perspectives, and countering the static nature of traditional training databases. This open version, however, should be restricted to *sophisticated users*—defined here as individuals with a legal background. This restriction is proposed to maintain the quality of the feedback loop. Sophisticated users, with their specialized knowledge and experience, are more likely to provide constructive and relevant feedback, which is crucial for the iterative

[5] https://www.harvey.ai/.

[6] https://go.lexisnexis.ca/lexis-plus-ppc-ai.

improvement of the system. By incorporating inputs from a diverse yet expert user base, the AI system can be continuously refined and updated, ensuring it remains relevant and effective in a rapidly evolving legal environment.

Note that feedback data provided by professionals will take many forms—(i) user behaviour, (ii) handwritten expert feedback, (iii) conversation steering, (iv) response ratings, (v) external feedback. All forms of data contribution by user-contributors, depicted in Fig. 3 through a platform called *OpenJustice*,[7] are a valuable resource, which can be useful for supervision in our framework. Additionally, databases in the unstructured format may potentially be valuable by incorporating in our framework through pretraining or domain-adaptation. However, the value of the aforementioned remains unexplored in the legal domain, and has been shown to not be useful in other domains such as finance [29].

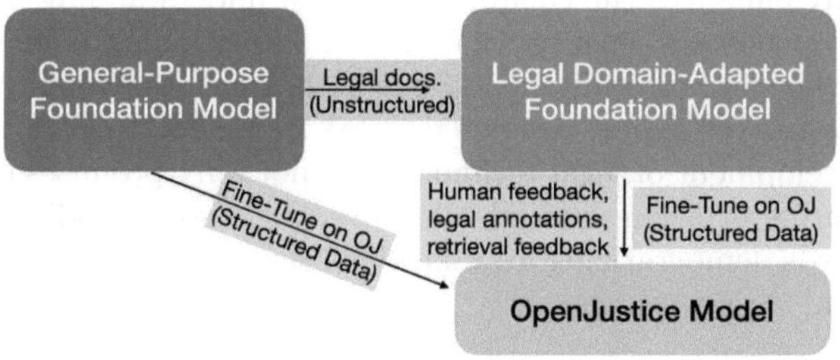

Fig. 3. Legal Community Feedback utilized for OpenJustice.

In the rapidly evolving field of artificial intelligence, particularly in the context of developing AI models for legal applications, a suite of advanced methodologies and research breakthroughs offer promising avenues. Direct Preference Optimization (DPO) [30], is particularly pertinent for legal AI due to its capability to align model outputs with complex, often subjective human preferences, a common characteristic in legal reasoning. This method's ability to refine AI outputs based on nuanced user feedback makes it exceptionally suited for the legal domain where interpretations and judgments are not always clear-cut. World models, as outlined in [23], offer another compelling tool for legal AI. These models enable the AI to create internal simulations of possible scenarios, an approach that mirrors the predictive and hypothetical reasoning often employed in legal analysis. By simulating various legal outcomes and scenarios, a world model-equipped legal AI can provide more comprehensive and informed suggestions. Advances like Flash Attention 2 [32] contribute significantly by enabling the processing of large volumes of legal texts efficiently. This efficiency is crucial in legal contexts, where the ability to rapidly parse through extensive legal documents and case laws is a valuable asset. Furthermore, techniques like rejection sampling and reward modeling are instrumental in refining the quality of

[7] https://openjustice.ai/.

AI-generated legal content. Rejection sampling can be used to filter out less relevant or lower-quality content, ensuring that the AI's outputs are pertinent and of high quality. Reward modeling aligns the AI's objectives with desired outcomes, an essential feature when the AI is required to navigate the complex landscape of legal ethics and standards. Lastly, supervised fine-tuning and alignment research are integral to the development of a legal AI model. Supervised fine-tuning allows the model to learn from specific, high-quality legal datasets, ensuring that its outputs are relevant and accurate. Alignment research, which focuses on ensuring that AI systems' goals are aligned with human values and intentions, is particularly critical in the legal domain, where the stakes of misalignment can be particularly high.

The integration of the aforementioned methodologies and research developments presents a comprehensive approach for training legal AI models. This integration not only enhances the capability of AI in understanding and processing legal information but also ensures that the AI's functioning is aligned with the nuanced, complex, and ethically bound nature of legal reasoning. Also, this proposed open-access, yet expert-restricted, legal AI model represents a paradigm shift in the development of legal technology. It not only promises enhanced performance in terms of accuracy and relevance but also embodies a progressive approach towards democratizing legal knowledge and fostering an inclusive legal tech ecosystem.

7 Conclusion

Artificial intelligence has been bringing a profound impact on legal applications. In this work, we bring a call for open-source legal language models. This is done as a means to address limitations of general-purpose language models which may have underlying limitations, affecting their usage for high-stakes decision making. We provide a recipe for creating a legal language model, called OpenJustice. We further introduce a real-world high-quality dataset manually annotated by legal experts, called LegalQA, and run experiments outlining performance of current state-of-the-art LLMs. We place further emphasis on highlighting the limitations in the automatic evaluation process when used on legal datasets.

Acknowledgements. We would like to thank students of the Conflict Analytics Lab at Queen's University Faculty of Law for being a part of initial efforts put into this initiative, and David Liang for coordinating efforts.

References

1. Touvron, H., et al.: LLaMA: open and efficient foundation language models (2023). https://arxiv.org/abs/2302.13971
2. Anil, R., et al.: Gemini: a family of highly capable multimodal models (2023). https://arxiv.org/abs/2312.11805

3. Shur-Ofry, M.: Multiplicity as an AI Governance Principle. Rochester, NY (2023). https://doi.org/10.2139/ssrn.4444354
4. Katz, D.M., Bommarito, M.J., Gao, S., Arredondo, P.: GPT-4 Passes the Bar Exam. Rochester, NY (2023). https://doi.org/10.2139/ssrn.4389233
5. Stiglitz, J.: Modeling Legal Reasoning: LM Annotation at the Edge of Human Agreement. Working Paper (2023)
6. Cohen, M.C., Dahan, S., Khern-Am-Nuai, W., Shimao, H., Touboul, J.: The use of AI in legal systems: determining independent contractor vs. employee status. Artif. Intell. Law 1–30 (2023)
7. Kleinberg, J., Ludwig, J., Mullainathan, S., Sunstein, C.R.: Discrimination in the age of algorithms. J. Legal Anal. **10**, 113–174 (2018). https://doi.org/10.1093/jla/laz001
8. Chen, Y., Andiappan, M., Jenkin, T., Ovchinnikov, A.: A Manager and an AI Walk into a Bar: Does ChatGPT Make Biased Decisions Like We Do? Rochester, NY (2023). https://doi.org/10.2139/ssrn.4380365.
9. Merken, S.: New York lawyers sanctioned for using fake ChatGPT cases in legal brief. Reuters (2023)
10. Choi, J.H., Hickman, K.E., Monahan, A., Schwarcz, D.: ChatGPT goes to law school (January 23, 2023). 71 J. Legal Educ. 387 (2022). SSRN: https://ssrn.com/abstract=4335905 or http://dx.doi.org/10.2139/ssrn.4335905
11. Blair-Stanek, A., Carstens, A.-M., Goldberg, D.S., Graber, M., Gray, D.C., Stearns, M.L.: GPT-4's Law School Grades: Con Law C, Crim C-, Law & Econ C, Partnership Tax B, Property B-, Tax B (2023). SSRN: https://ssrn.com/abstract=4443471 or http://dx.doi.org/10.2139/ssrn.4443471
12. Katz, D.M., Bommarito, M.J., Gao, S., Arredondo, P.: GPT-4 Passes the Bar Exam (2023). SSRN: https://ssrn.com/abstract=4389233 or http://dx.doi.org/10.2139/ssrn.4389233
13. Nay, J.J., et al.: Large language models as tax attorneys: a case study in legal capabilities emergence. arXiv preprint arXiv:2306.07075 (2023)
14. Blair-Stanek, A., Holzenberger, N., Van Durme, B.: OpenAI cribbed our tax example, but can GPT-4 really do tax?. arXiv preprint arXiv:2309.09992 (2023)
15. Medianik, K.: Artificially intelligent lawyers: updating the model rules of professional conduct in accordance with the new technological era. Cardozo L. Rev. **39**, 1497 (2017)
16. Green, B.A., Silver, C.: Technocapital@ Biglaw. com. Nw. J. Tech. & Intell. Prop. **18**, 265 (2020)
17. Martínez, E.: Re-evaluating GPT-4's bar exam performance. SSRN 4441311 (2023)
18. Martin, L., et al.: Better call GPT, comparing large language models against lawyers. arXiv:abs/2401.16212 (2024): n. pag
19. Law Geex: Comparing the performance of artificial intelligence to human lawyers in the review of standard business contracts. Law Geex (2018)
20. Rudin, C.: Stop explaining black box machine learning models for high stakes decisions and use interpretable models instead. Nat. Mach. Intell. **1**(5), 206–215 (2019)
21. Dahan, S., Touboul, J., Lam, J., Sfedj, D.: Predicting Employment Notice Period with Machine Learning: Promises and Limitations. McGill Law Journal (2020)
22. Markou, C., Deakin, S.: Ex Machina Lex: Exploring the Limits of Legal Computability. Rochester, NY (2019). https://doi.org/10.2139/ssrn.3407856.
23. Ha, D., Schmidhuber, J.: World models. In: Advances in Neural Information Processing Systems 31 (NeurIPS 2018) (2018). https://arxiv.org/abs/1803.10122

24. Bhambhoria, R., Dahan, S., Zhu, X.: Investigating the state-of-the-art performance and explainability of legal judgment prediction. In: Canadian Conference on AI (2021)
25. Luo, C.F., Bhambhoria, R., Dahan, S., Zhu, X.: Evaluating explanation correctness in legal decision making. In: Proceedings of the Canadian Conference on Artificial Intelligence (2022). https://doi.org/10.21428/594757db. 8718dc8b
26. Luo, C.F., Bhambhoria, R., Dahan, S., Zhu, X.: Prototype-based interpretability for legal citation prediction. arXiv (2023). https://doi.org/10.48550/arXiv.2305. 16490.
27. Hilton, J., Nakano, R., Balaji, S., Schulman, J.: WebGPT: improving the factual accuracy of language models through web browsing. OpenAI Blog **16** (2021)
28. Nakano, R., et al.: WebGPT: browser-assisted question-answering with human feedback. arXiv preprint arXiv:2112.09332 (2021)
29. Li, X., et al.: Are ChatGPT and GPT-4 general-purpose solvers for financial text analytics? A study on several typical tasks. arXiv preprint arXiv:2305.05862 (2023)
30. Rafilov, R., et al.: Direct preference optimization: your language model is secretly a reward model. arxiv preprint arxiv:2305.18290 (2023)
31. Surden, H.: Artificial intelligence and law: an overview. Georgia State University Law Rev. **35**(4) (2019)
32. Dao, T.: FlashAttention-2: faster attention with better parallelism and work partitioning. arxiv preprint arxiv:2307.08691 (2023)
33. Guha, N., et al.: LegalBench: prototyping a Collaborative Benchmark for Legal Reasoning. arxiv preprint arxiv:2209.06120 (2022)
34. Du, N., et al.: GLaM: efficient scaling of language models with mixture-of-experts. In: Proceedings of the 39th International Conference on Machine Learning, PMLR, vol. 162, pp. 5547–5569 (2022)
35. Magesh, V., et al.: Hallucination-Free? Assessing the reliability of leading AI legal research tools. arxiv preprint arxiv:2405.20362 (2024)
36. Little, S.: AI 'Hallucinated' Fake Legal Cases Allegedly Filed to B.C. Court in Canadian First. Global News (2024). https://globalnews.ca/news/10238699/fake-legal-case-bc-ai/. Accessed 25 Jan 2024
37. Dahl et al.: Large legal fictions: profiling legal hallucinations in large language models. arxiv preprint arxiv:2401.01301 (2024)
38. Chen, L., Zaharia, M., Zou, J.: How Is ChatGPT's behavior changing over time? Harvard Data Sci. Rev. **6**(2) (2024). https://doi.org/10.1162/99608f92.5317da47
39. Wu, S., et al.: BloombergGPT: a large language model for finance. arXiv preprint arXiv:2303, 17564 (2023)
40. Li, X., et al.: Are ChatGPT and GPT-4 general-purpose solvers for financial text analytics? A study on several typical tasks. In: Proceedings of the 2023 Conference on Empirical Methods in Natural Language Processing: Industry Track, pp. 408–422 (2023)
41. Mitra, A., et al.: Orca 2: teaching small language models how to reason. arXiv preprint arXiv:2311. 11045 (2023)

Evaluating University Curricula in Preparing Future AI Developers to Comply with the AI Act: A Case Study of Belgium

Valentina Dalla Giovanna[1,2], Gregory Lewkowicz[1,2](✉), and Anissa Mahloul[1]

[1] Smart Law Hub, Université Libre de Bruxelles, Avenue Franklin Roosevelt 50, 1050 Bruxelles, Belgium
gregory.lewkowicz@ulb.be

[2] FARI: AI for the Common Good Institute, ULB/ VUB, Cantersteen 16, 1000 Bruxelles, Belgium

Abstract. As the global regulatory landscape for AI expands, the EU has taken a pioneering step by adopting the AI Act. This act introduces new obligations for AI operators to promote trustworthy AI and ensure a high level of protection for health, safety, and fundamental rights. By setting requirements for placing AI systems and models on the market, the regulation is expected to impact the AI industry across Europe and beyond. While some of these obligations consolidate existing best practices, those related to fundamental rights and ethics are relatively new for the industry. These require AI developers to adapt their practices and foster a culture of compliance to avoid significant fines or even market exclusion. This paper explores whether future AI developers are being adequately prepared through their university curricula to meet the fundamental rights and ethical requirements set forth by the AI Act. It proposes a qualitative method for assessing the readiness of university programs in AI-related disciplines. This method is applied to all relevant curricula offered by the 10 universities in Belgium during the 2023–2024 academic year, evaluating 1562 courses across 95 programs. Findings reveal minimal exposure to fundamental rights and ethics, which undermines students' ability to integrate these values into their future professional roles. These highlight the responsibility of universities to strengthen their programs by more thoroughly integrating fundamental rights and ethics into the curricula for future generations of AI professionals.

Keywords: AI act · Trustworthy AI · Ethical AI · Fundamental rights · Computer science education · Compliance · Ethical requirements

1 Introduction

As artificial intelligence (AI) continues to permeate all aspects of our society, there is growing awareness of its potential threats to essential societal values enshrined in fundamental rights and ethics. Initiatives such as the OECD AI Principles [21],[1] UNESCO's

[1] Adopted in 2019 and updated in 2024.

© The Author(s), under exclusive license to Springer Nature Switzerland AG 2026
D. Restrepo Amariles and K. Satoh (Eds.): *Compliance for Artificial Intelligence Systems*, LNAI 14377, pp. 75–95, 2026.
https://doi.org/10.1007/978-3-032-12795-2_6

Ethics of AI Recommendation [24],[2] and the European Ethics Guidelines for Trustworthy AI (HLEG) [9],[3] all echo the same message: fostering AI that upholds fundamental rights and ethics is paramount. This trend reflects a global commitment to addressing ethical concerns throughout the entire AI lifecycle—from development to deployment and beyond—and is driving the progressive adoption of regulations worldwide.

In this context, the European Union (EU) has taken a pioneering step by adopting the world's first comprehensive regulation on AI, the AI Act [7], which came into effect on August 1, 2024. The act aims to promote the adoption of human-centric and trustworthy AI while ensuring a high level of protection for health, safety, and fundamental rights. It introduces new obligations for operators of AI systems and models throughout their lifecycle. Specifically, the act requires, in certain cases, producers of AI systems to undergo a conformity assessment—covering aspects of fundamental rights and ethics—before placing an AI system or model on the market or putting it into service. Producers that do not comply with the AI Act face severe consequences, including market bans, product recalls, and fines of up to €35 million or 7% of annual revenue.[4]

While some of the obligations established by the AI Act consolidate existing best practices, those related to fundamental rights and ethics are relatively new for the industry. They will require computer scientists, software engineers, and other AI professionals to adapt their practices and foster a culture of compliance. Without adequate preparation, they risk developing systems that fail to comply with European legal requirements and fall short of broader societal expectations for trustworthy AI.

The question then arises as to whether future AI developers are acquiring the necessary knowledge during their university training to develop artificial intelligence systems that comply with societal expectations and the European regulation in terms of respect for fundamental rights, sustainability and the broader societal impacts of AI. Adequate training is essential to ensure the successful commercialization of AI products and to drive the economic growth of the EU's AI industry. Non-compliance with these obligations poses significant risks to both commercialization efforts and the broader industry—challenges that stakeholders may not yet fully recognize. This article explores this question through a qualitative assessment of the coverage of fundamental rights and ethics in all relevant curricula offered by Belgium's 10 universities during the 2023–2024 academic year.

The paper is structured as follows. First, we review the current literature on integrating legal and ethical considerations into AI education. Second, we outline our research methodology. Third, we present our findings, analyzing the extent to which these programs prepare future AI professionals to develop trustworthy AI that aligns with fundamental rights and ethical standards. Finally, we summarize the key findings, discuss the limitations of our approach and opportunities for future improvement, and conclude with an exploration of the broader implications of these results.

[2] Adopted in 2021.

[3] Adopted in 2019.

[4] Articles 74 and 99 of the AI Act [7] and 14 of the Regulation (EU) 2019/1020 [9].

2 Literature Review

While the integration of ethics and fundamental rights into computer science education has garnered substantial scholarly interest, most of the literature focuses on the benefits of this integration or proposes methods to achieve it, rather than empirically assessing the extent to which these aspects are incorporated into current education.

O'Sullivan et al. [3] underscore ethics as central through the Ethics4EU project, which addresses key areas like privacy and algorithmic decision-making, while Brown et al. [5] advocate for best practices and effective teaching strategies. Furthermore, Goetze [17] adds that ethics integration can benefit from a multi-, inter-, or transdisciplinary approach. Appel and Miller [19] contend that technical computing issues are best understood within a social context, while the societal impacts of computing benefit from being grounded in technical detail. They show that including computer ethics in the curriculum not only enhances students' motivation but also deepens their understanding of the complex relationship between technology and society.

Fiesler, Garrett, and Beard [11] provide insights from a global analysis of 115 syllabi, highlighting diverse approaches and recommending further ethics integration while Orchard and Radke [22] show that engineering students generally struggle with AI ethics. Bezuidenhout et al. [4] developed an ethics curriculum for short data science courses at the CODATARDA Schools, emphasizing "open and responsible data science citizenship." Their approach incorporates virtue ethics to encourage ethical practices, helping students integrate ethics into their daily work in data science. Barnard et al. [23] emphasize educators' roles in cultivating ethical awareness, proposing a framework used at the University of South Africa. Similarly, Ferreira and Vardi [10] reflect on their experience with an "Ethics and Accountability" course at Rice University, and Kopec et al. [18] demonstrate that embedding ethics strengthens students' capacities to address ethical issues. Fiesler et al. [11] argue for embedding ethics in programming courses to confront students with real-world dilemmas from the start. Fischer-Hübner [14] specifically emphasizes privacy, outlining a structured approach for its teaching in German universities.

Research evaluating the extent to which computer science and related disciplines integrate training on fundamental rights and ethics remains limited. Saltz et al. [13] analyzed the syllabi of machine learning courses from a broad range of U.S. institutions and found that most programs do not include any ethics-related content. Similarly, Mbuki [20] conducted an extensive qualitative analysis of computer science courses in Kenya, concluding that ethical topics are seldom addressed. In Europe, Stavrakakis et al. [23] are among the few to have thoroughly explored this issue, finding that most European institutions allocate minimal hours to ethics in computer science education. However, their conclusions are based on a survey of only 61 respondents, limiting the generalizability of their findings.

Our study distinguishes itself from previous research in two ways. First, it goes beyond general ethics coverage to assess whether AI education equips students with the knowledge necessary to develop AI systems that meet societal expectations and comply with the AI Act, particularly in terms of respecting fundamental rights, promoting sustainability, and addressing the broader societal impacts of AI. Second, to our knowledge, it is the first comprehensive effort to evaluate the inclusion of ethics and fundamental rights education across all computer science programs at a national level. By analyzing 1562 courses across 95 programs in all Belgian universities offering such curricula, this study enables us to draw conclusions that are, in some respects, more systematic and representative.

3 Methodology

3.1 Research Methodology and Question

This study uses a qualitative approach to assess the extent to which fundamental rights and ethics are integrated into Belgian computer science and related education programs. The central question is whether Belgian universities adequately prepare future AI professionals to meet the EU's AI Act standards for trustworthy AI. We test two hypotheses: (1) that Belgian curricula insufficiently integrate the ethical and legal requirements stemming from the AI Act, and (2) that significant gaps exist between the AI Act's obligations and students' awareness of the foundational knowledge needed to meet them.

3.2 Rationale for the Qualitative Method

Given the challenges in assessing how well educational programs address the AI Act's complex technical obligations regarding fundamental rights and ethics, we have chosen to use the seven requirements of the HLEG as a proxy. This approach is justified by the AI Act's explicit references to these guidelines and by Article 95(2)(a), which identifies them as relevant guidance for all AI systems. However, we have excluded the requirement of 'robustness' from our study. While robustness is a critical and interdisciplinary element of computer science, it is more broadly integrated across various stages of education, making it difficult to evaluate on a course-by-course basis. Additionally, robustness is primarily a technical requirement, differing significantly from fundamental rights and ethics.

The six requirements that we have taken into account in the evaluation are: (1) Human agency and oversight including fundamental rights; (2) Privacy and data governance covering privacy, data integrity, and access; (3) Transparency addressing traceability, explainability and communication; (4) Diversity, discrimination and fairness focusing on avoidance of bias, accessibility and stakeholder participation; (5) Societal and environmental well-being incorporating sustainability, social impact and democracy, and (6) accountability involving auditability, reporting and redress mechanisms.

To evaluate the extent to which each course covers the different requirements, we adopted a qualitative approach that accommodates the interpretative nature of both course content and legal and ethical requirements. This approach provides the flexibility to assess whether requirement-related content is taught as a standalone subject, integrated within technical courses, or both, and enables us to distinguish between superficial mentions and more in-depth coverage.

3.3 Dataset and Data Collection Methods

Under two Belgian decrees,[5] universities are required to publish comprehensive descriptions for each course, including learning outcomes, course nature and content, teaching profile, and evaluation methods. For the programs we assessed, we collected all course information published in compliance with these decrees, which, in principle, includes descriptions of all courses taught in Belgium.

We identified the programs to be assessed by navigating each university's website. Using filters such as sciences, engineering, data science, and AI, we selected programs in computer science, engineering (e.g., civil, digital, data engineering, ICT), data science, and cybersecurity—core domains for AI development. We excluded more specialized fields such as bioinformatics, medical informatics, and disciplines like pure mathematics and statistics.

We limited our analysis to the 10 Belgian universities offering relevant programs: Universiteit Hasselt (UHasselt), Université Libre de Bruxelles (ULB), Université de Liège (ULiège), Université de Mons (UMons), Universiteit Gent (UGent), Université Catholique de Louvain (UCL), Katholieke Universiteit Leuven (KUL), Université de Namur (UNamur), Vrije Universiteit Brussel (VUB), and Universiteit Antwerpen (UAntwerpen) (see Fig. 1). Our focus was on Bachelor's and Master's programs from the 2023–2024 academic year, irrespective of the language of instruction (Dutch, French, or English). Programs were selected based on Bologna system standards, excluding specialized and non-standard offerings (see Tables 2 and 3).

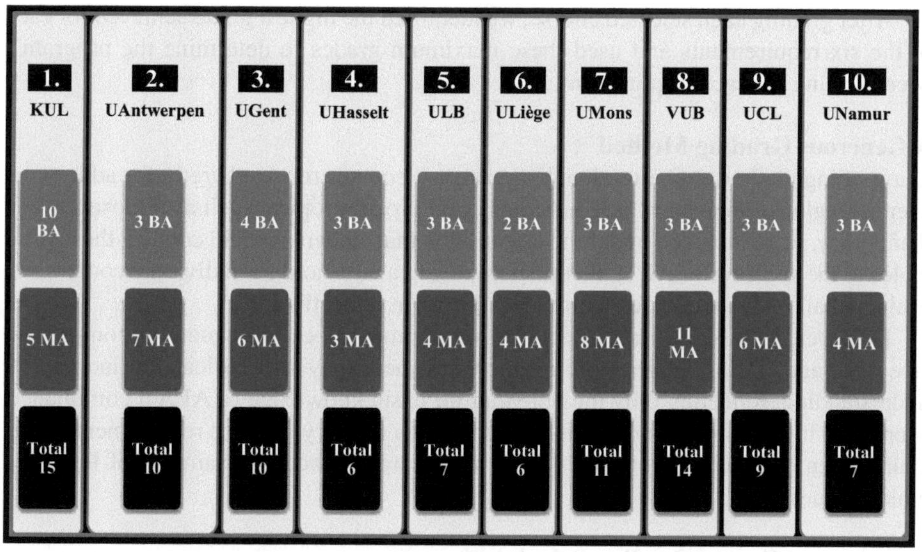

Fig. 1 Distribution of 95 Programs across 10 Universities

[5] Combined reading of Articles 124 and 77, Decree of 7 November 2013 defining the landscape of higher education and the academic organization of studies [16]; Combined reading of Articles II.220 and II.221, § 1, 4° et 5°, Codex of Flemish Higher Education of 11 October 2013 [15].

After selecting and evaluating 1562 courses, we found considerable overlap across programs offering the same courses, reducing the total to 668 unique courses. For programs jointly organized by multiple universities, we counted each instance separately, once for each university offering the program.

3.4 Data Analysis

The Grading Scale and General Evaluation Framework
Each course was evaluated based on a grading scale (0–4) applied to the six ethical requirements (see Table 1).

Table 1 The Grading scale applied to each of the six ethical requirements

Grade	Criteria
0	No coverage of the requirement.
1	Requirement addressed as a secondary focus in an elective course.
2	Requirement addressed as a secondary focus in a mandatory course.
3	Requirement addressed as a primary focus in an elective course.
4	Requirement addressed as a primary focus in a mandatory course.

After grading each selected course, we identified the highest grade achieved for each of the six requirements and used these maximum grades to determine the program's overall rating for each requirement.

A Generous Grading Method
Our grading method was intentionally generous: courses received credit for addressing even a single component of a requirement, and broader topics, such as philosophy and democracy, were included under the assumption that students would connect these principles to the specifics of AI. Rather than imposing a threshold for individual courses, we evaluated all relevant courses within each program collectively.

However, addressing one aspect of a requirement does not equate to comprehensive coverage. Thus, a high score in our assessment may still indicate an incomplete understanding, reflecting only the potential for basic knowledge of AI Act compliance. Moreover, high scores do not equate to a thorough mastery of these requirements especially when courses are not directly tied to concrete, practical examples of legal and ethical issues in AI.

The General Course Grading Principles
The general course grading principles are as follows. Courses with titles and content explicitly referencing ethical components, such as privacy or sustainability, received higher grades (3 or 4). In contrast, broader topics like philosophy were minimally graded, typically under societal well-being, and only when the course description aligned with one of the requirements' components. Courses focused specifically on ethics earned

maximum grades for societal well-being, while those mentioning ethics more peripherally received minimal grades for that requirement. Courses with variable content, such as guest lectures, were graded at the minimum for each relevant component. However, if most of the content aligned with societal well-being, they received the maximum grade for that category, with no grade assigned for other ethical requirements related to the variable content.

General references to discrimination, gender issues, migration, or inequality were graded under societal well-being unless they specifically focused on bias reduction, in which case they were evaluated under discrimination, diversity and fairness. Law courses that briefly covered fundamental rights received minimal grades for human agency and oversight (e.g., courses on Belgian law and legal systems). Finally, courses with insufficient detail in their titles or descriptions were assigned a grade of 0 across all requirements.

Specific Cases of Excluded Programs

Two specific programs were excluded from the analysis. The "Master of Applied Sciences and Engineering: Computer Science Multimedia" (a joint program offered by VUB and Northwestern Polytechnical University in China) was excluded due to insufficient information. The "Master in Computer Systems Architecture" was only graded for UNamur, as ULiège did not list this program on its website.

Grading Process

Each course was graded independently by two junior researchers. At the end of their grading process, they compared results and discussed any divergences. Discrepancies were resolved collegially. An expert was consulted in unresolved cases (e.g., this was the case for courses broadly addressing ethics). This dual-evaluator approach, with expert arbitration, when necessary, promoted consistent, well-reasoned grading and helped reduce risks of inconsistency and subjective bias.

4 Results

4.1 Assessing Belgian Programs by Requirement

Selected Bachelor Programs

The study evaluates requirement scores for 37 Belgian bachelor programs (see Figure 6). Nearly 11% (4 programs) meet none of the requirements, while 46% (17 programs) address only one. An additional 27% (10 programs) cover only two requirements, meaning 84% of programs address no more than two areas, indicating a limited educational scope. Notably, 43% of bachelor's programs provide training that covers more than a single requirement, even if only addressed peripherally.

All programs that cover at least one requirement include requirement 6 (Environmental and Societal Well-being). While Human Agency and Oversight are central to the AI Act—emphasized as a primary concern under Article 14—only about 14% of the programs incorporate this value, distributed across just 5 programs. Accountability is almost absent, represented in only one program (less than 3% of the course offerings). Additionally, only around 19% of the offerings (7 programs) address Diversity, non-discrimination, fairness. The limited emphasis on transparency is troubling; only 4 programs (about 11% of the course offerings), include it, despite this principle being a cross-cutting requirement and obligation for compliance with the AI Act. Privacy and data governance, another important area, are included in only 22% of the offerings (8 programs).

To conclude, these findings illustrate the overall trend of limited coverage across bachelor programs. VUB's Bachelor of Science in Artificial Intelligence stands out, covering five requirements and scoring 18 out of 24. UGent's Bachelor in de industriële wetenschappen (informatica) follows, covering four requirements and scoring slightly above the minimum threshold with a total of 13 out of 24. All other programs fall below the average, with a top score of 10 out of 24, achieved by programs from UGent, UNamur, and UCL, each covering only three requirements. The Bachelor in Civil Engineering Sciences (Charleroi) includes no relevant courses.[6] Most relevant courses are elective, and no single course fully meets all requirements.

Overall, these findings reveal substantial gaps, with only 3% of bachelor programs offering a well-rounded curriculum. This raises concerns about bachelor students' preparedness to meet AI Act standards and apply ethical AI practices, as most programs remain narrowly focused.

Selected Master Programs

The analysis of 58 master's programs reveals a stronger alignment with the AI Act's core requirements compared to bachelor's programs, though key gaps remain (see Fig. 7). Societal and Environmental Well-being is the most frequently covered requirement, addressed in 54 programs (93%), followed closely by Privacy and Data Governance in 48 programs (83%). Diversity, Non-Discrimination, and Fairness appears in 35 programs (60%), while Transparency is included in 26 programs (45%). However, Human Agency and Oversight is represented in only 16 programs (28%), and Accountability remains the least addressed, covered by just 15 programs (26%).

In terms of overall coverage, most master's programs address only a limited number of requirements: 2 programs (3%) cover none, 6 programs (10%) cover one, and 14 programs (24%) cover only two. Notably, 53% of programs address no more than three requirements, and 66% cover up to four, indicating that few programs offer a comprehensive curriculum aligned with all AI Act principles. Only 14 programs (24%) score above 12 out of 24, while 6 programs (10%) reach a score of exactly 12 out of 24.

Notably, the master's programs at ULiège consistently achieve high scores, defying the overall trend by covering all ethical requirements with grades of 18/24 or 24/24. This strong performance is largely attributed to a single course, "European Law, (Big) Data, and AI Seminar," which addresses the relevant legislative framework, including the AI Act. Depending on the program, this course may be optional or mandatory, resulting in slight grading variations.

[6] This bachelor's degree was selected because its counterpart offered in Brussels was also included for the same university.

4.2 Evaluating Ethical Standards in Belgian University Programs

Distribution of Average and Median Requirements Grades at the Bachelor's Level by Belgian University

Figures 2 and 3 (see hereunder) provide a comprehensive overview of the legal and ethical requirements addressed in bachelor's programs across Belgian universities, displaying respectively both the mean and median values for each requirement.

This figure highlights the most frequently addressed requirements within each University and presents the overall scores for each university, ordered from highest to lowest mean. The universities, ordered from lowest to highest mean scores, are ULiège, ULB, UMons, KUL, UNamur, UHasselt, UAntwerpen, UCL, UGent and VUB (See Fig. 2). Most universities address only a single requirement— Environmental and Societal Well-being—with other ethical topics largely underrepresented. Across all institutions, the average mean scores barely reach 5.55 out of 24.

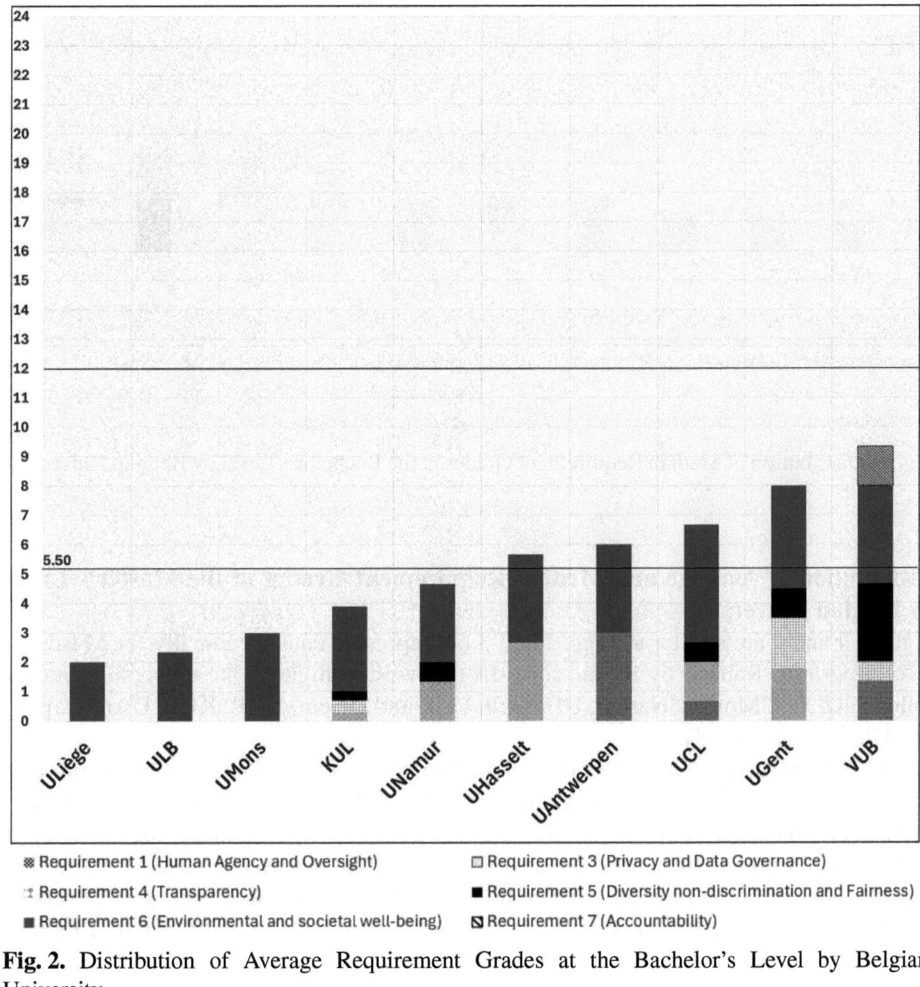

Fig. 2. Distribution of Average Requirement Grades at the Bachelor's Level by Belgian University.

On average, all universities (10 out of 10) include Societal and Environmental Well-being in their bachelor's programs. Privacy and Data Governance and Diversity, Non-Discrimination, and Fairness are covered by 5 out of 10 universities. Human Agency and Oversight and Transparency is addressed by only 3 out of 10 universities (see Fig. 2).

In terms of median for bachelor's programs within a single university, 6 out of 10 Universities only focus on Societal and Environmental Well-being, while 3 out of 10 cover two requirements, and just 1 out of 10 addresses four requirements. This distribution indicates that, in terms of the median, 90% of the university's bachelor programs incorporate no more than two of the six core ethical requirements (see Fig. 3).

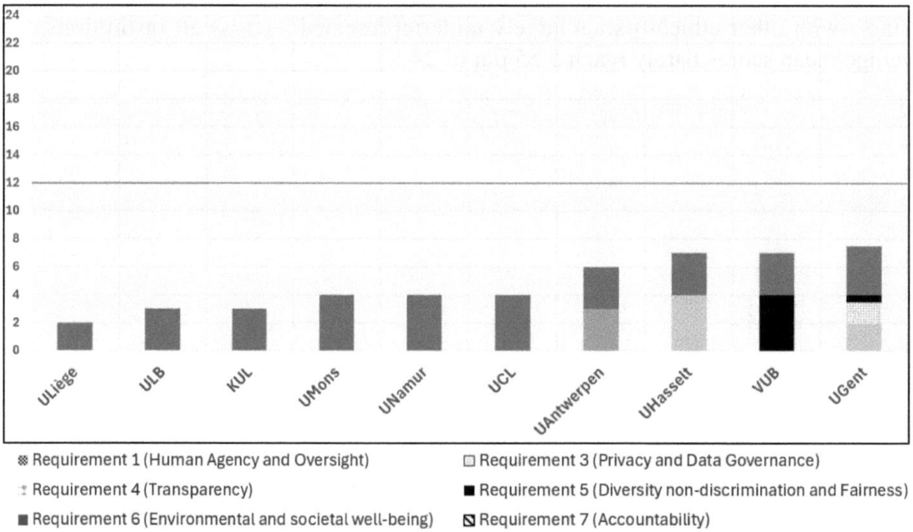

Fig. 3 Distribution of Median Requirement Grades at the Bachelor's Level by Belgian University

Distribution of Average and Median Requirement Grades at the Master's Level by Belgian University

Figures 4 and 5 are similar to Figs. 2 and 3 but represent data specifically for Master's-level programs. Ranked by mean scores from lowest to highest, the universities are as follows: ULB, UMons, UNamur, UHasselt, UCL and UGent, VUB, KUL, UAntwerpen, and ULiège (see Fig. 4).

Across universities, all (10 out of 10) address Diversity, Non-Discrimination, and Fairness at the mean level as well as Environmental and societal well-being, with Privacy and Data Governance being included by 9 out of 10 institutions. Transparency is covered by 6 out of 10 universities, Accountability by 5, and Human Agency and Oversight by only 4. These figures illustrate that although certain requirements, such as Diversity and Privacy, are widely integrated, others like Human Agency and Oversight remain underrepresented.

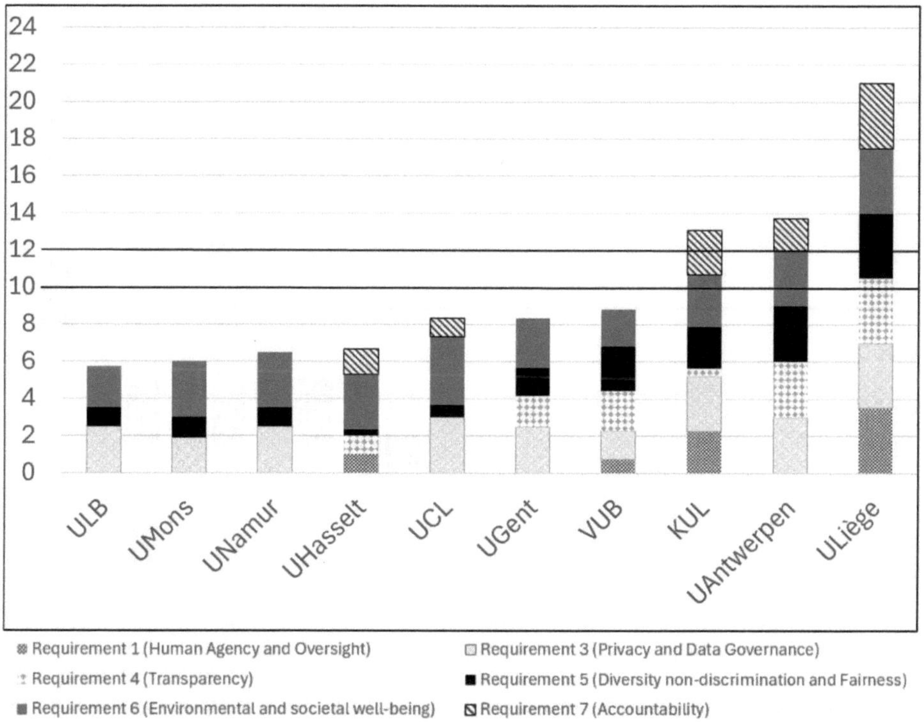

Fig. 4. Distribution of Average Requirement Grades at the Master's Level by Belgian University.

In terms of median distribution, 1 out of 10 universities addresses only a single requirement, 3 out of 10 include only two requirements, 1 out of 10 covers three requirements, 1 out of 10 covers four, and another 3 out of 10 address five. This means that, at the median, 50% of universities cover a maximum of three requirements, and 60% only cover a maximum of four requirements (see Fig. 5).

At ULiège, both the mean and median scores reach 21 out of 24, as shown in Figs. 4 and 5, indicating comprehensive coverage of all requirements. UAntwerpen follows with an average score of 13.71 out of 24. KUL has an average score of 13.08 out of 24, while the remaining universities fall significantly lower, with average scores below 9 out of 24 (see Fig. 4). Despite ULiège's high scores, the overall average across all institutions remains low, with a global mean of 9.82 out of 24. This highlights a widespread, limited emphasis on ethical requirements among Belgian master's programs.

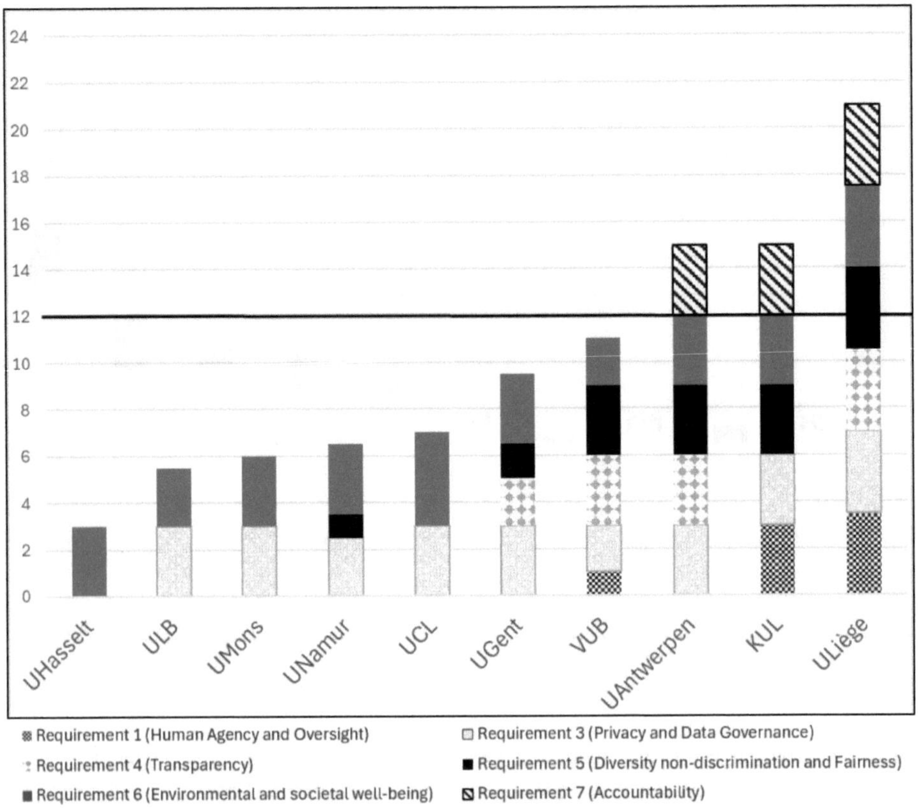

Fig. 5. Distribution of Median Requirement Grades at the Master's Level by Belgian University.

5 Conclusion

The study's empirical approach provides valuable insights but is limited by several factors. A primary limitation is the transparency of course content. Many universities do not fully comply with the legal obligation to publish detailed course descriptions, restricting the analysis to course titles. This lack of transparency potentially introduces biases and errors, as titles alone cannot accurately convey the scope or depth of requirements covered. In this context, our decision to consider general ethical or philosophical courses as fulfilling partially the societal and environmental well-being requirement may have led to an overestimation of the actual coverage of this requirement. Future research could mitigate this issue by directly obtaining syllabi or interviewing faculty members to clarify the content taught, ensuring a more accurate assessment.

Other limitations are related to the macro-level approach used, as it evaluates program offerings without considering individual student choices, the practical accessibility of specific courses, or whether courses sufficiently cover all requirements. The methodology does not account for the instructional hours dedicated to each requirement, allowing a single course to disproportionately influence a university's overall score. A finer-grained, micro-level analysis would enrich these findings by examining whether students can realistically complete the ethical requirements and how well program offerings align with their actual experiences. Such an approach could provide a more nuanced understanding of the situation and reveal potential gaps between program objectives and student outcomes.

While acknowledging these limitations, the study generally confirms both of our hypotheses. Despite the generous grading criteria, students across all universities and program levels seem to receive extremely minimal exposure to ethics and fundamental rights standards, underscoring a lack of basic preparation to build compliance capacity for the AI Act. Bachelor's programs average around 6/24, and master's programs around 10/24. Societal and Environmental Well-being and Privacy are the most frequently covered topics; however, Human Agency and Oversight and Accountability remain notably lacking across most institutions.

Bachelor's programs show considerable deficiencies, with 84% covering no more than two requirements. Master's programs offer somewhat broader coverage, though 60% still address a maximum of four ethical requirements.

ULiège stands out with its comprehensive coverage, achieving a mean score of 21/24 across its master's programs, largely due to a single course. The significant impact of a single course on the overall result is consistent with our chosen method; however, this should be interpreted with caution, as it is unlikely that a single course can adequately cover all six requirements in sufficient depth.

Currently, almost none of the programs in Belgium equip students with basic knowledge to address fundamental rights and ethical issues. Conducting similar studies at the European level would be valuable to determine whether these findings can be generalized and reflect the broader European context. These results highlight the responsibility of universities to strengthen their programs by more thoroughly integrating fundamental rights and ethics into the curricula for future generations of AI professionals. Preparing future computer scientists is essential, as they will shape the AI industry of tomorrow. Without adequate training, future AI professionals will be unable to foster a culture of compliance within the industry or align AI systems and models with core societal values. This could hinder the commercialization of AI products and the broader growth of the EU's AI industry. Universities should ensure that future computer scientists are adequately educated to facilitate the development and commercialization of AI systems within the EU market while upholding fundamental rights and ethical values.

Building on these findings, future research should assess the curricula for future AI professionals across Europe using a similar methodology to determine whether our results are representative of the broader state of higher education in the Union. Future research could also explore the feasibility of developing standardized checklists or guidelines at the EU level, which universities could use to validate their curricula in terms of the inclusion of fundamental rights and ethics. Such efforts would support evidence-based decision-making and necessary harmonization of educational approaches, which are crucial for ensuring the development of trustworthy AI in Europe and the proper implementation of the AI Act.

Acknowledgments. We thank contributors to the consolidation of the dataset of the Smart Law Hub, especially Simone Casalena, Driss El Qaisy and Tom De Clercq. All errors are the sole responsibility of the authors.

Disclosure of Interests The authors have no competing interests to declare that are relevant to the content of this article.

Appendices

Appendix 1: List of the University Programs Selected

Table 2 Selected Bachelor's Programs List

University	Program	Our Code
ULB	Bachelier en sciences informatiques	ULB-B1
	Bachelier en sciences de l'ingénieur, orientation ingénieur civil (option Bruxelles)	ULB-B2
	Bachelier en sciences de l'ingénieur, orientation civil (option Charleroi)	ULB-B3
ULiège	Bachelier en sciences informatiques	UL-B1
	Bachelier en sciences de l'ingénieur, orientation ingénieur civil	UL-B2
UHasselt	Bachelor handelsingenieur in de beleidsinformatica	UH-B1
	Bachelor in de industriële wetenschappen	UH-B2
	Bachelor in de informatica	UH-B3
UCL	Bachelier en sciences de l'ingénieur, orientation ingénieur civil	UCL-B1
	Bachelier en sciences informatiques (Charleroi)	UCL-B2
	Bachelier en sciences informatiques (LLN)	UCL-B3
UMONS	Bachelier en sciences de l'ingénieur (Charleroi)	UM-B1
	Bachelier en sciences de l'ingénieur (Mons)	UM-B2
	Bachelier en sciences informatiques	UM-B3
VUB	Bachelor in de Computerwetenschappen	VUB-B1
	Bachelor in de artificiële intelligentie Standaard traject	VUB-B2
	Bachelor of science in de Wiskunde en data science	VUB-B3
KUL	Bachelor in de industriële wetenschappen (Brugge)	KUL-B1
	Bachelor in de industriële wetenschappen (Geel)	KUL-B2
	Bachelor in de industriële wetenschappen (gent)	KUL-B3
	Bachelor in de industriële wetenschappen (Leuven)	KUL-B4
	Bachelor in de industriële wetenschappen (Sint-Katelijne-waver)	KUL-B5
	Bachelor in de industriële wetenschappen (Diepenbeek)	KUL-B6
	Bachelor in de informatica (Leuven)	KUL-B7
	Bachelor in de informatica (Kortrijk)	KUL-B8

(continued)

Table 2 (*continued*)

University	Program	Our Code
	Bachelor in de ingenieurswetenschappen (Leuven)	KUL-B9
	Bachelor of engineering technology (Leuven)	KUL-B10
UGent	Bachelor of science in de informatica	UG-B1
	Bachelor of science in de industriële wetenschappen (elektronica-ICT)	UG-B2
	Bachelor of science in de industriële wetenschappen (informatica)	UG-B3
	Bachelor of science in de ingenieurswetenschappen (computerwetenschappen)	UG-B4
UAntwerpen	Bachelor Informatica	UA-B1
	Bachelor Handelsingenieur in de beleidsinformatica	UA-B2
	Bachelor Industriële wetenschappen: Elektronika-ICT	UA-B3
UNamur	Bachelier en sciences informatiques (Charleroi)	UN-B1
	Bachelier en sciences informatiques	UN-B2
	Bachelier en sciences informatiques (horaires décalés)	UN-B3

Table 3 Selected Master's Programs List

University	Program	Our Code
ULB	Master in cybersecurity	ULB-M1
	Master en sciences informatiques à finalité Spécialisée	ULB-M2
	Master: Ingénieur civil en informatique à finalité Spécialisée	ULB-M3
	Master: Ingénieur civil en informatique à finalité big data management and analytics (Erasmus mundus)	ULB-M4
ULiège	Master en science des données, à finalité	UL-M1
	Master: Ingénieur civil en science des données, à finalité	UL-M2
	Master: Sciences informatiques, à finalités	UL-M3
	Master: Ingénieur civil en informatique à finalité	UL-M4
UHasselt	Master handelsingenieur in de beleidsinformatica	UH-M1
	Master in de informatica	UH-M2
	Master of statistics and data science	UH-M3
UCL	Master: Ingénieur civil en informatique	UCL-M1
	Master: Ingénieur civil en science des données	UCL-M2
	Master en science des données, orientation statistiques	UCL-M3
	Master en science des données, orientation technologies de l'information	UCL-M4
	Master en sciences informatiques	UCL-M5

(*continued*)

Table 3 (*continued*)

University	Program	Our Code
	Master in cybersecurity (ULB)	UCL-M6
UMONS	Master en mathématiques à finalité spécialisée: Métiers de l'informatique et de l'intelligence artificielle (Mons)	UM-M1
	Master en sciences informatiques à finalité approfondie (Mons)	UM-M2
	Master en sciences informatiques à finalité spécialisée (Mons)	UM-M3
	Master en sciences informatiques, à finalité spécialisée professionnelle (Charleroi)	UM-M4
	Master en sciences informatiques, à finalité spécialisée en artificial intelligence and data analytics (Mons)	UM-M5
	Master: Ingénieur civil en informatique et gestion, à finalité spécialisée en ingénierie logicielle et business intelligence (Charleroi)	UM-M6
	Master: Ingénieur civil en informatique et gestion, à finalité spécialisée en cybersecurity and forensics for the internet of everything (Mons)	UM-M7
	Master: Ingénieur civil en informatique et gestion, à finalité spécialisée en artificial intelligence and decision aid (Mons)	UM-M8
VUB	Master in applied sciences and engineering: Computer science Standaard traject	VUB-M1
	Master in de ingenieurswetenschappen: Toegepaste computerwetenschappen	VUB-M2
	Master of science in applied sciences and engineering: Computer science artificial intelligence	VUB-M3
	Master of science in applied sciences and engineering: Computer science data management and analytics	VUB-M4
	Master of science in applied sciences and engineering: Computer science multimedia	VUB-M5
	Master of science in applied sciences and engineering: Computer science software languages and software engineering	VUB-M6
	Master of science in de Ingenieurwetenschappen: Computerwetenschappen afstudeerrichting Artificiële Intelligentie	VUB-M7
	Master of science in de Ingenieurwetenschappen: Computerwetenschappen afstudeerrichting data management en analytics	VUB-M8
	Master of science in de Ingenieurwetenschappen: Computerwetenschappen afstudeerrichting multimedia	VUB-M9
	Master of science in de Ingenieurwetenschappen: Computerwetenschappen afstudeerrichting software languages and software engineering	VUB-M10
	Master of science in de Ingenieurwetenschappen: Elektronica en Informatietechnologie	VUB-M11

(*continued*)

Table 3 (*continued*)

University	Program	Our Code
KUL	Master in de ingenieurswetenschappen: Computerwetenschappen	KUL-M1
	Master in de ingenieurswetenschappen: Wiskundige ingenieurstechnieken	KUL-M2
	Master of engineering: Computer science	KUL-M3
	Master of statistics and data science (on campus)	KUL- M4
	Master of statistics and data science (blended)	KUL-M5
UGent	Master of science in de informatica	UG-M1
	Master of science in business engineering (data analytics)	UG-M2
	Master of science in computer science engineering	UG-M3
	Master of science in de ingenieurswetenschappen: Computerwetenschappen	UG-M4
	Master of science in de ingenieurswetenschappen: Elekrotechniek	UG-M5
	Master of science in electrical engineering (communication and information technology)	UG-M6
UAntwerpen	Master informatica: Computernetwerken	UA-M1
	Master informatica: Data science en artificiële inteligentie	UA-M2
	Master informatica: Software engineering	UA-M3
	Master of computer science: Data science and artificial intelligence	UA-M4
	Master in computer science: Software engineering	UA-M5
	Master in computer science: Computer network	UA-M6
	Master in digital business engineering	UA-M7
Université de Namur	Master en sciences informatiques, à finalité spécialisée en data science	UN-M1
	Master en sciences informatiques, à finalité spécialisée en software engineering	UN-M2
	Master en architecture des systèmes informatiques, à finalité spécialisée (codiplôme avec l'Haute-Ecole Namur-Liège-Luxembourg et l'Université de Liège)	UN-M3
	Master in cybersecurity (ULB)	UN-M4

Appendix 2: Grades Assigned to each Programs

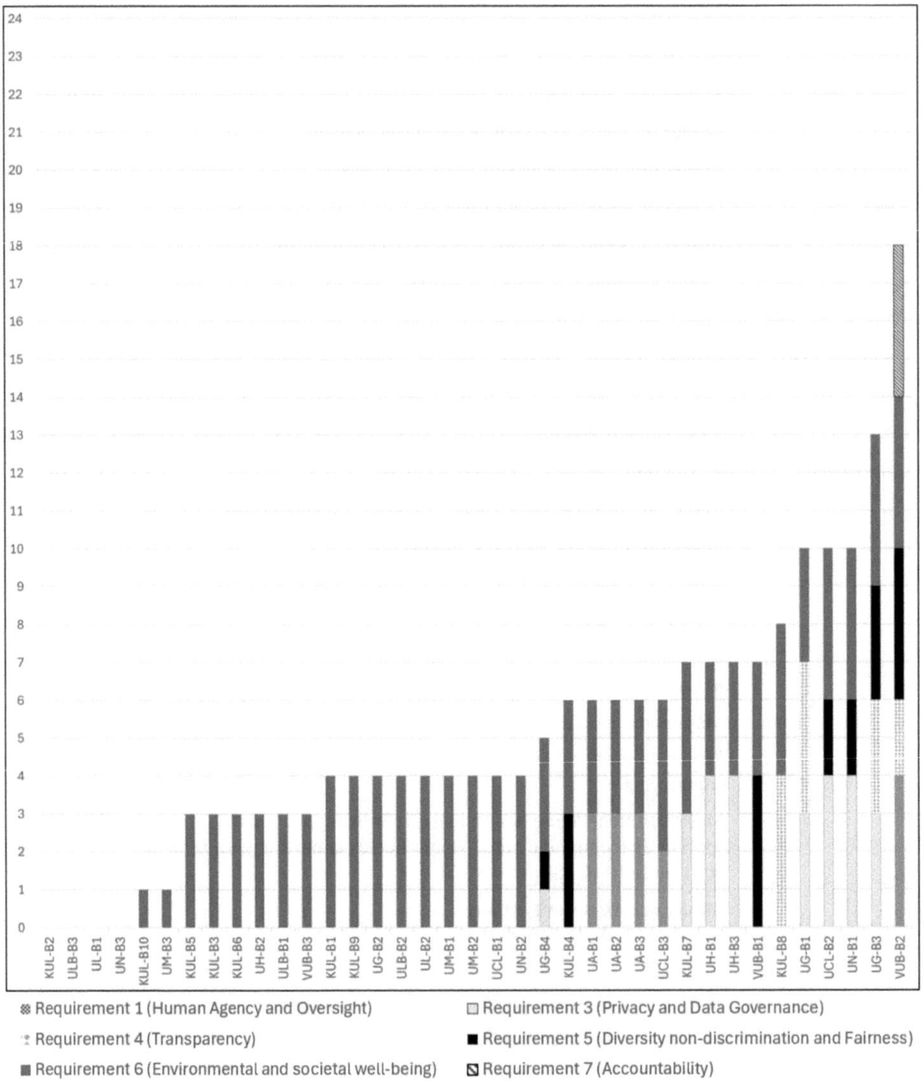

Fig. 6. Grades assigned to each Bachelor Program

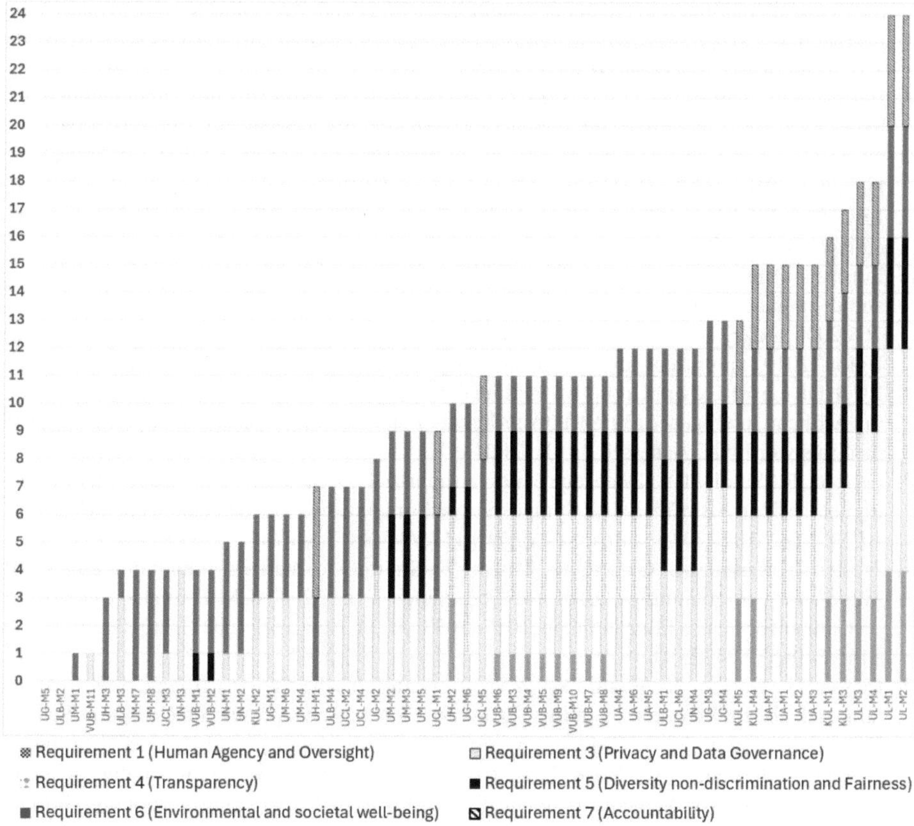

Fig. 7. Grades Assigned to each Master Programs

References

1. Appel, F., Miller, K.W.: Introducing computer ethics into the computer science curriculum. Comput. Sci. Educ. **1**(1), 37–52 (2001). https://doi.org/10.1080/0899340880010104
2. Barnard, A., de Ridder, C., Pretorius, L., Cohen, E.: Integrating computer ethics into the computing curriculum: a framework for implementation. In: Proceedings of the 2003 InSITE, Vol. 3, pp. 265–279 (2003). https://doi.org/10.28945/2619
3. Becevel, A., Curley, A., Gibson, J.P., Gordon, D., Murphy, E., O'Sullivan, D.: Ethics4eu: designing new curricula for computer science ethics education: case studies for Ai ethics. European Society for Engineering Education. (2023). https://doi.org/10.21427/5yyb-6h60
4. Bezuidenhout, L., Shanahan, H., Quick, R.: Ethics when you least expect it: a modular approach to short course data ethics instruction. Sci. Eng. Ethics. **26**, 2189–2213 (2020). https://doi.org/10.1007/s11948-020-00197-2
5. Brown, N., Xie, B., Sarder, E., Fiesler, C., Wiese, E.S.: Teaching ethics in computing: a systematic literature review of ACM computer science education publications. ACM Trans. Comput. Educ. **24**(1), 1–36 (2024). https://doi.org/10.1145/3634685
6. European Commission: Explanatory Memorandum to COM(2021)206 on the Proposal for a Regulation of the European Parliament and of the Council laying down Harmonised Rules

on Artificial Intelligence (Artificial Intelligence Act) and Amending Certain Union Legislative Acts (2021). https://eur-lex.europa.eu/legal-content/EN/TXT/?uri=COM%3A2021%3A0206%3AFIN. Accessed 01 NOV 2024
7. European Parliament and Council Regulation (EU) 2024/1689 of 13 June 2024 laying down harmonised rules on artificial intelligence and amending Regulations (EC) No 300/2008, (EU) No 167/2013, (EU) No 168/2013, (EU) 2018/858, (EU) 2018/1139 and (EU) 2019/2144 and Directives 2014/90/EU, (EU) 2016/797 and (EU) 2020/1828 (Artificial Intelligence Act). 12 July 2024. 2024/1689, Official Journal of the European Union (2024). https://eur-lex.europa.eu/legal-content/EN/TXT/?uri=CELEX:32024R1689. Accessed 01 Nov 2024
8. European Parliament and of the Council, Regulation (EU) 2019/1020 on market surveillance and compliance of products and amending Directive 2004/42/EC and Regulations (EC) No 765/2008 and (EU) No 305/2011. 20 June 2019. 2019/1020, Official Journal of the European Union (2019). https://eur-lex.europa.eu/eli/reg/2019/1020/oj/eng
9. EU High-Level Expert Group on Artificial Intelligence: Ethics Guidelines for Trustworthy Artificial Intelligence (2019). https://digital-strategy.ec.europa.eu/en/library/ethics-guidelines-trustworthy-ai. Accessed 31 Oct 2024
10. Ferreira, R., Vardi, M.Y.: Deep tech ethics: an approach to teaching social justice. In: Proceedings of the 52nd ACM Technical Symposium on Computer Science Education, pp. 1041–1047. ACM, New York (2021). https://doi.org/10.1145/3408877.3432449
11. Fiesler, C., Friske, M., Garrett, N., Muzny, F., Smith, J.J., Zietz, J.: Integrating ethics into introductory programming classes. In: Proceedings of the 52nd ACM Technical Symposium on Computer Science Education, pp. 1027–1033. ACM, New York (2021). https://doi.org/10.1145/3408877.3432510
12. Fiesler, C., Garrett, N., Beard, N.: What do we teach when we teach tech ethics? A syllabi analysis. In: Proceedings of the 51st ACM Technical Symposium on Computer Science Education, pp. 289–295. ACM, New York (2020). https://doi.org/10.1145/3328778.3366825
13. Fiesler, C., Gorelick, M., Saltz, J., Skirpan, M., et al.: Integrating ethics within machine learning courses. ACM Trans. Comput. Educ. **19**(4), 1–26 (2019). https://doi.org/10.1145/3341164
14. Fischer-Hübner, S.: Teaching privacy as a part of the computer science curriculum. In: Katz, Y.J., Millin, D., Offir, B. (eds.) The Impact of Information Technology IFIP Advances in Information and Communication Technology, pp. 47–56. Springer, Boston (1996). https://doi.org/10.1007/978-0-387-35061-5_5
15. Flemish Community, Codex of Flemish Higher Education of 11 October 2013. February 27 2014, Moniteur Belge (2014). http://www.ejustice.just.fgov.be/eli/decreet/2013/10/11/2014A35166/justel
16. French Community, Decree of 7 November 2013 defining the landscape of higher education and the academic organization of studies. January 1 2014, Moniteur Belge (2014). https://www.ejustice.just.fgov.be/eli/decret/2013/11/07/2013029625/justel. Accessed 01 Nov 2024
17. Goetze, T.S.: Integrating ethics into computer science education: multi-, inter-, and transdisciplinary approaches. In: Proceedings of the 54th ACM Technical Symposium on Computer Science Education, Vol. 1, pp. 645–651. ACM, New York (2023). https://doi.org/10.1145/3545945.3569792
18. Kopec, M., et al.: The effectiveness of embedded values analysis modules in computer science education: an empirical study. Big Data Soc. **10**(1), 1–13 (2023). https://doi.org/10.1177/20539517231176230
19. Miller, K.: Integrating computer ethics into the computer science curriculum. Comput. Sci. Educ. **1**(1), 37–52 (1988). https://doi.org/10.1080/0899340880010104
20. Mbuki, K.: Curriculum analysis: the state of ethics in computer science curriculum in Kenyan universities. Int. J. Comput. Trends Technol. (2023)

21. OECD: Recommendation of the Council on Artificial Intelligence, OECD/LEGAL/0449 (2019). https://legalinstruments.oecd.org/en/instruments/OECD-LEGAL-0449#mainText. Accessed 01 Nov 2024
22. Orchard, A., Radke, D.: An analysis of engineering students' responses to an AI ethics scenario. Proc. Thirty Seventh AAAI Conf. Artif. Intell. **37**(13), 15834–15842 (2024). https://doi.org/10.1609/aaai.v37i13.26880
23. Stavrakakis, I., Gordon, D., Tierney, B., et al.: The teaching of computer ethics on computer science and related degree programmes. A European survey. Int. J. Ethics Educ. **7**(2), 101–129 (2021). https://doi.org/10.1007/s40889-021-00135-1
24. UNESCO: Recommendation on the Ethics of Artificial Intelligence (2021). https://unesdoc.unesco.org/ark:/48223/pf0000381137. Accessed 01 Nov 2024
25. Zaidan, E., Ibrahim, I.A.: AI governance in a complex and rapidly changing regulatory landscape: a global perspective. Humanit. Soc. Sci. Commun. **11**(1), 1–18 (2024). https://doi.org/10.1057/s41599-024-03560-x

GPT Adoption Dilemma and the Impact of Disclosure Policies

Cathy Yang, David Restrepo-Amariles, Leo Pick Allen, and Aurore Clément Troussel(✉)

HEC Paris, Jouy–en–Josas, France
{yang,restrepo-amariles}@hec.fr, {leo.allen,aurore.troussel}@hec.edu

Abstract. Generative Pre-trained Transformers (GPTs), particularly Large Language Models (LLMs) like ChatGPT, have proven effective in content generation and productivity enhancement. However, legal risks associated with these tools lead to adoption variance and concealment of AI use within organizations. This study examines the impact of disclosure on ChatGPT adoption in legal, audit and advisory roles in a professional service firm through the lens of agency theory. We conducted a survey experiment to evaluate agency costs in the context of unregulated corporate use of ChatGPT, with a particular focus on how mandatory disclosure influences information asymmetry and misaligned interests. Our findings indicate that in the absence of corporate regulations, such as an AI policy, firms may incur agency costs, which can hinder the full benefits of GPT adoption. While disclosure policies reduce information asymmetry, they do not significantly lower overall agency costs due to managers undervaluing analysts' contributions with GPT use. Finally, we examine the scope of existing regulations in Europe and the United States regarding disclosure requirements, explore the sharing of risk and responsibility within firms, and analyze how incentive mechanisms promote responsible AI adoption.

Keywords: Human-GPT collaboration · GPT disclosure · Agency theory · Content evaluation · Survey experiment

1 Introduction

The rapid adoption of generative artificial intelligence technologies, driven by advanced Large Language Models (LLMs) such as GPT, Claude, and Mistral, presents organizations with unprecedented opportunities. However, it also introduces complex legal and risk management challenges that demand careful consideration. A landmark ruling by the Hamburg Labor Court (Arbeitsgericht Hamburg) on January 16, 2024, addressed one of those crucial legal questions: Does an employer engage in employee monitoring when allowing the use of ChatGPT in the workplace via personal accounts? The Court ruled that as long as the employer has no knowledge of which employees are using ChatGPT, when,

© The Author(s), under exclusive license to Springer Nature Switzerland AG 2026
D. Restrepo Amariles and K. Satoh (Eds.): *Compliance for Artificial Intelligence Systems*, LNAI 14377, pp. 96–125, 2026.
https://doi.org/10.1007/978-3-032-12795-2_7

how, or to what extent, no monitoring occurs [1]. This ruling brings attention to a broader challenge, as organizations often struggle to monitor whether and how employees are using generative AI tools. We define the undisclosed use of AI tools in the workplace as "shadow adoption." To systematically analyze this issue, we propose using agency theory as an analytical framework.

Despite the expanding body of literature and experiments aimed at understanding the impact of generative AI in the workplace, there is a notable lack of empirical research analyzing this impact through the lens of agency theory. This gap is surprising, as the principal-agent problem can elucidate several critical issues identified in current research. These issues include the motivations and contexts under which employees adopt tools like ChatGPT [7,13,40], the conditions that give rise to specific legal risks and strategies for managing these risks [9,25,26], and the types of monitoring systems and incentives that can be implemented to promote the responsible use of generative AI in firms [28].

In this article, we argue that examining the adoption of ChatGPT and similar generative AI software in the workplace through the lens of the principal-agent problem offers valuable insights for developing effective corporate AI policies. Such policies are essential for managing legal risks and promoting responsible AI usage [10], addressing the core dilemma of balancing AI adoption with controlling associated risks. Our framework specifically highlights the organizational risks associated with individual and team-level adoption of generative AI within professional service firms. By analyzing the principal-agent relationship, we investigate how key factors—namely, information asymmetry, moral hazard, and incentives—shape the risks emerging from the adoption of ChatGPT and generative AI in firms. Accordingly, we later discuss why corporate AI policies are necessary to address these issues and how they can leverage solutions proposed in the agency literature. Specifically, we explore the implementation of control measures, incentive mechanisms, and risk management strategies as effective approaches.

The literature widely acknowledges that an agency relationship is established when a principal hires an agent to perform tasks on the principal's behalf [22,29,50]. The principal-agent scholarship focuses on addressing issues that arise from this relationship. These issues typically stem from three fundamental assumptions in agency theory [4,20]. First, issues arise from a misalignment of interests, wherein agents prioritize their self-interest over the objectives of principals [4,27]. Second, problems also emerge due to information asymmetry, as agents, who are the primary task performers, possess more information than principals [3,50]. Third, discrepancies in risk preferences between principals and agents lead to divergent actions (moral hazard), with agents generally exhibiting greater risk aversion compared to principals [4,27]. Agency theory posits that effective monitoring and incentive structures are essential for addressing these issues and ensuring risk-sharing that aligns the agent's risk attitudes and behaviors with the principal's interests [19,29,35,45]. While the implementation of monitoring and incentive mechanisms constitutes agency costs for the principal

[20], principals may prefer to incur these expenses rather than face potentially higher costs associated with diminished work quality and inadequate risk management.

Agency theory frequently conceptualizes the relationship between principals and agents using the metaphor of a contract [19,29,30]. Through this contract, the principal delegates tasks and decision-making authority to the agent [29, p. 308]. This perspective aligns with the modern theory of the firm, which defines firms as a nexus of contracts, where production results from coordinated efforts of a group of individuals [5,22]. Within this nexus, the ultimate principal is the shareholder, and the executives are the agents. Further down the line, managers and employees are linked by principal-agent relationships throughout the production chain [32]. As Zeckhauser notes, whenever one individual depends on the actions of another to produce value, an agency relationship arises: "The consultant is the agent, the client the principal. The absence of a formal contractual agreement directly binding managers and employees does not impede the establishment of a principal-agent relationship [46], as they are functionally interconnected and linked through the nexus of contracts constituting the firm. In other words, the contracting relationship between principal and agent may be either implicit or explicit [29, p. 308].

The chain of agency relationships within the corporation has been extensively discussed in legal scholarship [6,18,32]. Langevoort provides a thorough examination of what he terms "agency law within the corporation" to elucidate the duties of employees throughout the organization through the lens of principal-agent relationships. He highlights the intra-corporate duty of candor, which defines the duty owed by the board of directors to the shareholders, as well as by subordinates to their superiors [32]. According to Langevoort, this duty is essential for ensuring that critical information flows upwards to the board of directors, enabling them to be accountable to the shareholders. Consequently, corporate officers and employees are bound by an obligation that extends beyond merely avoiding falsehoods; they have an affirmative duty to disclose pertinent information. This obligation includes delivering all information relevant to the superior's decision-making, including any risks known to the employee [32, p. 2111].

Relationships where firms hire professional service organizations, such as consulting, auditing, and law firms, to carry out specific technical tasks are well-documented as principal-agent exchanges [20,36,44]. However, this article focuses on the internal dynamics between employees within the same professional service firm, particularly consulting firms tasked with delivering services to external clients, including strategic business advice, legal support, and auditing services. In this context, the agency relationship is established between a principal—an employee of the consulting firm who defines and assigns tasks and decisions—and an agent, another employee hired by the consulting firm to execute these tasks under the principal's direction.

One distinctive feature of agency relationships in consulting firms is the involvement of knowledge workers [37,44]. Unlike machine work, the success of knowledge-based organizations hinges on the abilities and expertise of their employees, who generate valuable ideas and knowledge that are not always easy to control. For example, managers may delegate specialized tasks to team members, such as financial, legal, or data analysis. Team members, acting as agents, use their knowledge and skills to complete these tasks, producing outputs that heavily depend on their specific competencies. As Mitchell and Meacheam state, following [44, p. 759] "the most significant difference between traditional agency exchanges and those involving knowledge workers is that, where a knowledge worker is the agent, division of labor is also a division of knowledge" [37, p. 151]. Characterizing the principal-agent relationship in consulting firms as a knowledge agency relationship highlights the specific input, effort, that agents are expected to provide to the principal as part of their incentive contract. In this context, effort is the intentional expenditure of personal (cognitive) resources directed toward achieving a valued outcome, which is costly, imperfectly observable, and shaped by rewards and monitoring [23]. Thus, that characterization anticipates the role that ChatGPT and similar technologies can play in exacerbating existing principal-agent problems.

In this article, we specifically analyze the dynamics between managers in legal, audit, and advisory roles, and their subordinates, which include both junior lawyers, analysts, and consultants, particularly focusing on scenarios where these subordinates utilize ChatGPT to perform their tasks. We conceptualize this dynamic as the manager-agent relationship. Within this framework, subordinates act as agents under the supervision of managers, who serve as principals, with the goal of delivering services to the firm's partners and clients. By interpreting the manager-subordinate relationship through the lens of agency theory, we scrutinize the operational and legal risks created by the agents' adoption of ChatGPT, focusing on information asymmetry and moral hazard. Additionally, we examine why AI corporate policies are essential for effectively addressing these novel risks and identify the specific issues these policies should consider.

First, the agent's use of ChatGPT may exacerbate information asymmetry between the principal and agent, particularly when the manager is unaware of the agent's reliance on ChatGPT. Without this knowledge, managers cannot implement additional controls to ensure the quality, authenticity, and originality of the work produced. The management literature and this study consistently show that managers have a hard time distinguishing between work produced by consultants with and without the assistance of ChatGPT due to the human-like text generated from ChatGPT [11,17]. Consequently, this new form of information asymmetry impedes managers' ability to assess well-established risks associated with ChatGPT, such as confidentiality breaches and misinformation. Finally, managers also lack information about the extent and types of interactions between the agent and ChatGPT, making it difficult to monitor the effort produced by the agent and the quality of the production process, let alone the process and quality of the outputs of ChatGPT itself.

Second, agents using ChatGPT may engage in behaviors that are not in the principal's best interest, thereby introducing moral hazard. Moral hazard arises because agents may prefer to exert less effort if all other factors remain constant [27]. While the principal might be indifferent to the agent's effort level if their share of benefits remains unchanged, they may nonetheless be exposed to additional, unrecognized risks. For instance, agents might opportunistically use ChatGPT to complete tasks quickly without substantial personal effort, given that managers still perceive the output quality favorably. Managers, unaware of the extent of ChatGPT usage, might erroneously assume that analysts are dedicating significant time and effort to their tasks, and pass on wrong information on costs to the partners and the client. The agent's risk preferences also differ from those of the principal. Agents may be more inclined to take risks, such as sharing confidential information with ChatGPT or incorporating ChatGPT-generated content into deliverables, if the principal is unaware of its use and cannot distinguish the source of the output. This misalignment in risk preferences and information can lead to suboptimal outcomes for the firm. Specifically, while consultants may benefit from the efficiency gains of using ChatGPT, the firm bears the risks associated with misinformation and confidentiality breaches.

The potential for high-risk exposure and monitoring costs could prevent managers in consulting firms from adopting enterprise-wide GPT despite its benefits. This conjecture is consistent with recent literature indicating that individuals' low adoption rate of LLM in the workplace is primarily attributed to restrictions on use from their superiors [28], which highlights that corporate adoption of GPT largely relies on the incentives of the principal (manager) among the principal-agent dyad to adopt GPT that aligns with the interests of the agents (analysts).

Traditional technology acceptance model suggests that technology adoption is positively driven by potential users' perceived usefulness and negatively influenced by perceived risk associated with the technology [2,12,47]. Despite the perceived usefulness with manageable risks under the recent technological advancements in AI, extensive literature documents individuals' aversion to its adoption [15,34], especially when the applied field is more subjective than objective [8], or when the individual is more experienced with the task [13,33]. Enhancing algorithmic transparency is one critical method to promote AI adoption. Transparency in AI is defined by disclosure in its usage, data handling, and decision-making processes [31,41]. While existing empirical studies show that increased algorithmic transparency could encourage adoption by enhanced decision accountability [24], trust [48], perceived fairness [16], and task efficiency [43], other studies find the opposite due to information overload [41,49] and reduced trust [15]. It is, therefore, unclear whether increasing transparency via subordinates' disclosure of the GPT use could encourage managers' adoption of GPT, which we empirically investigate in this study.

Prior research about GPT adoption focuses on individual-level adoption without considering the corporate hierarchies [13,39]. Yet, discussing the superiors' (managers') incentive to adopt GPT is challenging without considering implications for the subordinates contracted to perform specific tasks. When managers act as principals in a principal-agent dyad, subordinates' disclosure of GPT use implies reduced information asymmetry. Managers incur less information disadvantage regarding whether GPT participated in content generation. While this reduced information asymmetry could imply incentives for managers to allow GPT use at the workplace, it could challenge the current contract enforcing knowledge exchange between superiors and subordinates and thus incur agency costs. First, managers allowing GPT usage accompanied by subordinates' disclosure could imply misattribution of the effort subordinates exerted on a task, given its outcome with GPT participation. Thus, this disincentivizes subordinates to adopt GPT or disclose GPT use. Second, disclosure of GPT use increases the subordinates' accountability in managing risk in content production [22,42], which entails misinformation produced by GPT because of hallucinations and customers' confidentiality breaches due to subordinates' personal GPT usage. In sum, subordinates' disclosure of GPT reduces information asymmetry in a principal-agent dyad. Still, it is unclear whether it would better align the incentives between the manager and their subordinates in a workplace where the availability of GPT disrupts contract enforcement through increased content risk and uncertainties in effort exerted by subordinates, which calls for an empirical investigation.

In this study, we aim to empirically investigate whether subordinates' disclosure could encourage managers to adopt GPT (i.e., allowing subordinates to use GPT for content generation) in a context where there is no explicit regulation in the corporate AI policies. Additionally, we investigate whether analysts' disclosure of GPT use changes the incentive alignment of the manager-analyst dyad. In particular, we try to provide a nuanced understanding of the trade-offs involved in disclosure practices and their effectiveness in mitigating risks related to misinformation, confidentiality breaches, and the overall quality of work produced by ChatGPT agents. By exploring these dynamics, we contribute valuable insights into designing and implementing corporate AI policies that can better manage emerging risks preventing the adoption of generative AI in professional service firms.

2 Survey Experiment and Data

2.1 Study Overview and Design

Our objective is to explore whether analysts' disclosure of the GPT use that potentially reduces information asymmetry and mitigates risk could encourage managers' adoption of GPT in a consulting firm. There are several challenges to exploring this issue causally. First, we must collaborate with a consulting firm that hasn't adopted the GPT for the enterprise because any existing corporate-wide adoption could distort managers' preference for adoption. Second, to allow perfect counterfactual, we also need to enable some managers within a consulting firm to be randomly exposed to the disclosure of GPT use and some not by minimizing the spillover of treatment. Third, the analysts' choice to disclose GPT use needs to be out of the control of the managers to avoid endogeneity introduced by analysts' self-selection and their expectations of how managers react to GPT usage. Fourth, researchers also need to know whether analysts actually used GPT in content generation, which could be close to impossible due to the human-like nature of the GPT output, yet crucial to understanding the extent of information asymmetry induced by GPT usage. Following this point, managers also need to evaluate content generated by analysts with and without GPT to understand the extent of information asymmetry on an individual level. These challenges make achieving our core research objective in a natural field setting difficult, if not impossible.

To address these challenges, we collaborated with a major consulting firm that regulates the use of GPT at work (e.g., prohibiting employees from including their clients' information in prompts) to conduct a survey experiment. The firm's mid-level managers in legal, audit and advisory roles were enrolled in a training session to help them understand how they can benefit from generative AI to provide data-driven solutions for their potential clients. These mid-level managers often create pitch content with the help of their analysts in response to request-for-proposals (RFPs), which call for projects from potential new clients [21]. We simulate a critical part of this content co-creation process where managers contract analysts to draft initial pitch content, a research brief, in response to an RFP without knowing the actual content generation process unless disclosed. The experimental design randomly assigns managers to different rooms during their training sessions to evaluate the research briefs drafted by the analysts. One room of managers is assigned a survey link containing the pitch content without disclosing the source, while the other room is assigned a different survey link that discloses the content generation source (for both no-GPT and human-GPT generated content). Managers' physical separation would enforce the disclosure variation in the survey content to prevent treatment contamination due to the potential leak of deck generation source information if the managers were seated in the same classroom.

To further enforce the analysts' choice to disclose GPT out of the control of the managers, we hired two master's students with previous experience in consulting from a top European business school as junior analysts. The two analysts had no prior interaction with the managers, so they could create the content without knowing the managers' preference for content generation with or without GPT. We developed four RFPs with fictitious client names to increase the generalizability of our findings regarding the business topic in the interest of the consulting firm. Following a general structure of research brief in response to RFPs, each research brief comprised six sections: a problem statement, solution overview, implementation details, expected outcomes, team, and timeline. We obtained the ground truth of the content generation source by first instructing the two analysts to create research briefs collaboratively without using any LLMs, which they named the "No-GPT deck." After completing the four No-GPT decks, we asked the analysts to use ChatGPT 3.5, the version of the GPT model available for personal use at the time of the experiment, to modify the No-GPT decks without any specific instructions on how to prompt ChatGPT, which they named "Human-GPT deck."[1] It took the two analysts 38.5 h with 17€ per hour wage to finish generating the eight decks (four No-GPT decks and four Human-GPT decks), ranging from six to 11 pages each.

To ensure that GPT contributed to the content difference between the No-GPT and Human-GPT deck, we requested the analysts document their prompts and GPT responses by exporting their interactions with ChatGPT. The two analysts used 138 prompts before finalizing the four Human-GPT decks. Figure 5 shows the number of prompts used to update the content across the six content sections (problem statement, solution overview, implementation details, expected outcomes, team, and timeline). The prompt details are shown in Fig. 1. We categorized the prompts into four categories based on their application purpose: summarizing, expanding, inferring, and transforming according to [38], with additional categories of general advice-seeking and 'uncategorized' when the purpose of the prompt is hard to identify.

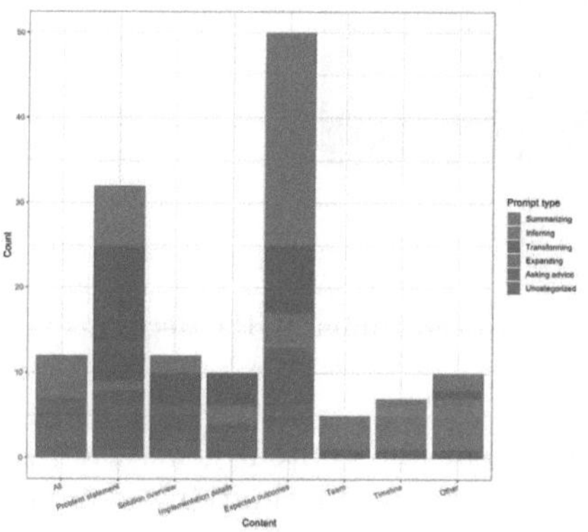

(a) Count

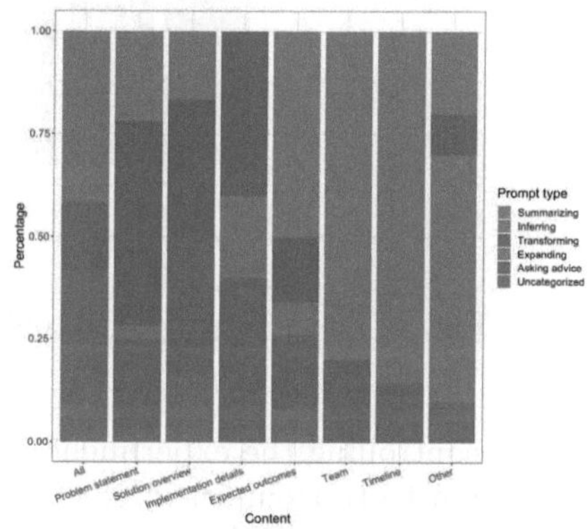

(b) Percentage

Notes: We classify the content category of a prompt in following categories: a whole (labeled as "all") when analysts demanded general assistance, one of the six sections (problem statement, solution overview, implementation details, expected outcomes, team, and timeline), or other content such as titles.

Fig. 1. Type of prompt used in each content generation section

We identify the contribution of GPT to the Human-GPT deck by the absolute differences in content similarity between the two versions of the brief (No-GPT

[1] Note that generating human-GPT collaborative content requires a longer time than the human-generated content by our design because the total effort amounts to the number of hours analysts spent building the non-GPT deck plus the interactions with GPT. This suggests an underestimation of effort exerted in the Human-GPT deck if managers perceived equal or less time in the content generation by analysts using GPT versus not.

and Human-GPT decks) and GPT responses. The content similarity between a deck and GPT responses is defined by the cosine similarity based on the text tokens using BERT tokenization ranging from 0 to 1, where a higher number indicates higher content similarity [14]. Figure 2 shows the degree of GPT contribution to the content in the Human-GPT (versus the No-GPT) deck, which suggests that the Human-GPT deck content results from analysts incorporating the GPT responses.

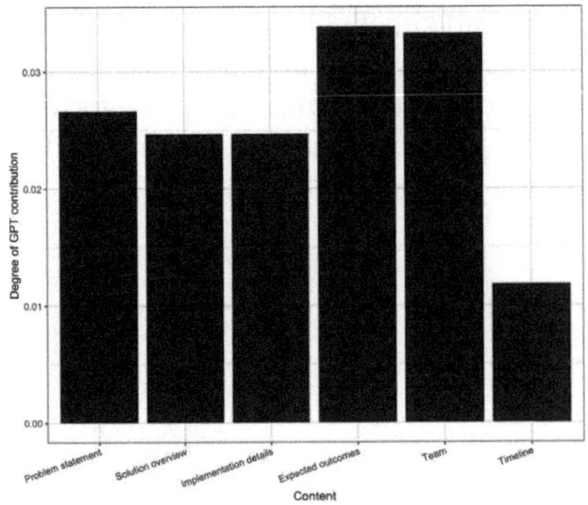

Fig. 2. The degree of GPT contribution to the Human-GPT deck.

After controlling the experimental environment and content generation process, we aim to test empirically: 1) whether there's an information asymmetry that managers cannot identify analysts' use of GPT in generating the research brief without an enforced disclosure policy, and whether GPT disclosure could reduce such information asymmetry; 2) the incentives (mis)alignment in GPT adoption and its disclosure among the manager-agent dyad. We thus adopt a mixed experimental design that combines within-subject and between-subject designs. The between-subject design focuses on the disclosure of content generation sources (no-GPT or human-GPT), compared to no such disclosure. The within-subject design involves each manager evaluating the No-GPT and Human-GPT versions of the research brief for a specific RFP. To identify the potential information asymmetry of analysts' GPT use, we measure managers' belief in analysts' GPT use before and after evaluating a research brief generated with or without GPT under different experimental conditions varying in its disclosure policy. Additionally, we assess analysts' incentives (disincentives) to adopt GPT and disclose its use through managers' evaluations of research brief quality (performance) and their subjective evaluation of the level of effort analysts exerted (perceived effort) with and without GPT use [42]. In particular, several scenarios exist: 1) analysts have a greater incentive to adopt and disclose GPT use when managers consider the research brief to be of better quality, and this much-improved quality is attributed to their more significant effort that translates to higher wages; 2) analysts have a greater incentive to adopt without disclose GPT use (i.e., shadow adoption) when managers consider the research brief to be of better quality, but the improved quality is not attributed to their effort; 3) analysts have no incentive to adopt GPT if the managers do not perceive a quality gain after using GPT for content generation. We define incentive alignment following a disclosure policy when it simultaneously encourages GPT adoption by the manager and analyst.

The detailed experimental procedure is described in the following section.

2.2 Experimental Procedure

One hundred thirty mid-level managers from a major consulting firm were involved in the training program about using generative AI to provide data-driven solutions across two sessions. All managers were randomly assigned to two classrooms for a training session (90 min and 60 min in the first and second waves, respectively). Before starting the training session, all managers were told about their mission to evaluate the research brief generated by two junior analysts in response to RFP from potential clients anonymously. In the first round of data collection, two out of four RFPs were randomly selected for each manager; in the second round, one out of four RFPs was chosen randomly.

Before proceeding to the deck evaluation section, we asked all managers for their estimates on the percentage likelihood that the two junior analysts would use GPT to develop research briefs. Understanding these prior beliefs helps eliminate potential confounding factors regarding how differences in those initial beliefs affect their post-belief perceptions of content generation sources—following disclosure or lack thereof.

In the deck evaluation section, managers assessed the No-GPT and Human-GPT decks created in response to an RFP, presented in a randomized order. In one classroom, managers were informed about the source of the content generation for the deck (Non-GPT and Human-GPT), while those in another classroom did not receive this information. For each RFP research brief deck, managers rated the content quality using three items on a scale from one to seven, as shown in Table 5 (Cronbach alpha = 0.78). Furthermore, we requested that the managers estimate how many hours they believed the deck generation required from the two analysts to reflect their perceived effort exerted by the analysts.

Following the presentation of the two decks for each research brief, managers were requested to express their beliefs in the junior analysts utilizing GPT for the No-GPT and Human-GPT decks. We asked managers to indicate their familiarity with the RFP process on a scale from one to five to assess their experience, as previous research shows that experience significantly influences an individual's appreciation or aversion to adopt an algorithm [13,33].

Following the evaluation of the deck, we assessed managers' tendencies to adopt GPT by their views on the GPT's perceived usefulness and risks [2,12,47]. We asked participants to rate the perceived usefulness (three items on a scale from one to seven as shown in Table 5, with a Cronbach alpha of 0.78) and the perceived risk (two items on a scale from one to five as displayed in Table 5, with a Pearson correlation of 0.43) of using GPT to create a research brief. Managers also indicate their preference to authorize junior analysts to use GPT when preparing a research brief for each of the six content sections (i.e., the problem statement, solution overview, implementation details, expected outcomes, team, and timeline) on a scale of one to five. We allow heterogeneity in managers' GPT adoption preferences across different content sections due to variations in how analysts use GPT, as shown in Figs. 5 and 2.

Before proceeding to the end of the survey, the managers were also asked to provide their demographic information, including gender, whether their role in the consulting firm involved facing the clients directly, tenure in the consulting industry, and average weekly working hours (less than 45 h, between 45 and 50 h, between 50 and 60 h, greater than 60 h).

Figure 3 summarizes the experimental procedure.

2.3 Data and Randomization Check

Ninety-two managers completed the survey experiment successfully. Among the 92 managers, 43 were informed about the source of the content generation, while 49 were unaware. We conducted a binomial test on the between-subject assignment outcome and found no significant difference in the frequency of managers assigned to the source transparency condition with 0.5 ($p = 0.47$).

Table 1 displays the summary statistics of the variables used in the main analysis, with the explanations of the variables shown in Table 6.

Table 1. Summary statistics

	Mean	Std Dev	Min	Max	Observations
SecGPTAuth	2.518	1.29	1	5	552
DeckQuality	4.478	1.02	1.50	7	238
DeckHour	15.77	27.4	0	200	238
IndNoGPTDeckFirst	0.511	0.50	0	1	92
IndExperience	1.672	0.95	1	4	92
IndGPTUsefulness	5.082	1.31	1	7	92
IndGPTRisk	4.571	0.69	2	5	92
IndFemale	0.391	0.49	0	1	92
IndClientFacing	0.696	0.46	0	1	92
# Prompts	4.83	6.06	1	27	24

We conduct a randomization check on the individual-level variables. First, we find no statistically significant difference in managers' *prior* beliefs about analysts' GPT use before evaluating the decks ($M_{No-Disclosure} = 44.9$, $M_{Disclosure} = 44.9$, $p = 1.00$ given a two-sample Student's t-test).

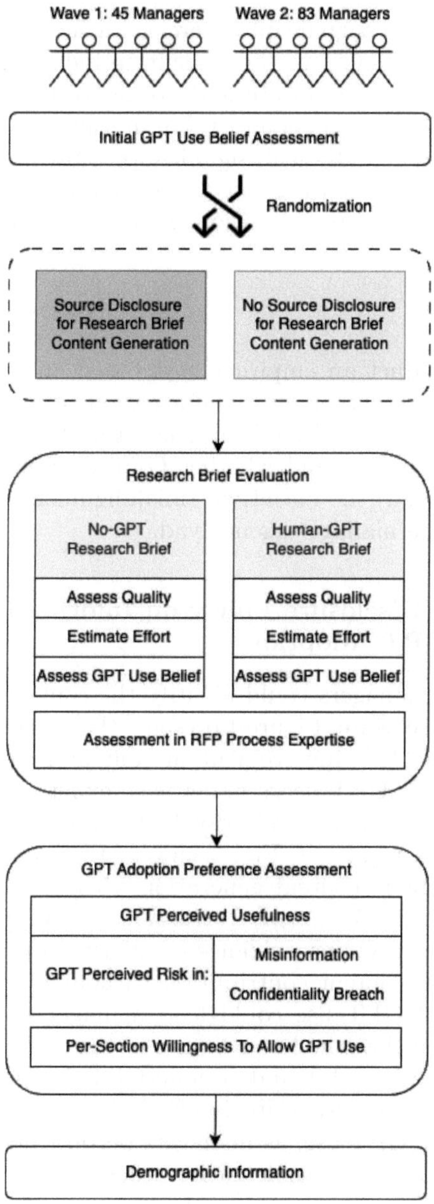

Fig. 3. Experimental procedure.

There is no statistically significant difference in the proportions of managers with a client-facing role, tenure in the consulting industry, and average weekly working hours between the disclosure and no disclosure conditions ($ps > 0.10$ given a Chi-square test of independence). We find proportionately more female managers with marginal statistical significance ($M_{No-Disclosure} = 30.61\%$, $M_{Disclosure} = 48.84\%$, $p = 0.07$ given a Chi-square test of independence) in the disclosure (vs. no-disclosure) condition, which we control for in the analyses.

3 Main Results

In this section, we conduct an empirical test based on our survey experiment to understand: 1) whether there's an information asymmetry that managers cannot identify analysts' use of GPT in generating the research brief without an enforced disclosure policy, and whether GPT disclosure could reduce such information asymmetry; 2) the incentives (mis)alignment in GPT adoption and its disclosure among the manager-agent dyad.

3.1 Impact of the Disclosure Policy on Information Asymmetry in Analysts' GPT Adoption

We first test whether managers could identify the content created by analysts' use of GPT without disclosure. Figure 4 presents the average percentage of managers who believe in GPT's involvement in content generation *after* evaluating Human-GPT and No-GPT decks under each experimental condition. While there was no difference in managers' prior belief in GPT's participation before content evaluation, the results in Fig. 4 suggest that managers could not discern GPT's involvement in content generation when its source is not disclosed ($M_{Human-GPT} = 77.55\%$, $M_{No-GPT} = 73.47\%$, $p = 0.68$ given a Chi-squared test of independence), providing evidence of information asymmetry regarding GPT's participation in content contribution without disclosure. Notably, analysts' non-disclosure of GPT use could lead managers, in general, to suspect their use of GPT, given that the lower bound of the 95% confidence intervals is above 50% for both the No-GPT and Human-GPT decks.

We find that enforcing disclosure is effective in reducing the information asymmetry of analysts' GPT use, as managers become better at identifying the content generated with GPT's participation when such information is disclosed ($M_{Human-GPT} = 83.72\%$, $M_{No-GPT} = 44.19\%$, $p < 0.001$ given a Chi-squared test of independence). Interestingly, 44.19% of the time, managers still think analysts used GPT despite full transparency and honesty about the lack of GPT use. This partially resulted from the managers' lack of trust in the analysts, given our experimental setting, where managers could not hand-pick their analysts to form a team. Nevertheless, it suggests a more significant reduction in information asymmetry if managers could trust analysts' honest disclosure of GPT use.

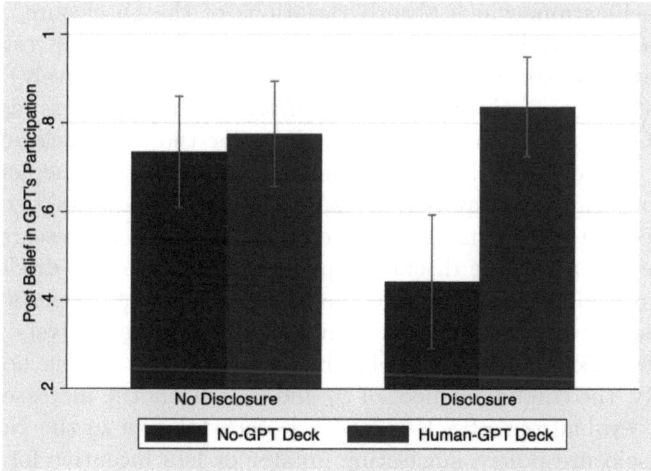

Note: The error bars indicate 95% confidence intervals.

Fig. 4. Managers could not identify analyst's use of GPT unless disclosed. Note: The error bars indicate 95% confidence intervals.

3.2 The Impact of Disclosure Policy on the Alignment in GPT Adoption Between the Manager-Agent Dyad

The information asymmetry between analysts and managers regarding GPT's participation in content generation without enforcement of disclosure policies suggests a potential moral hazard. Analysts may benefit from productivity gains achieved through GPT usage while exposing managers to risks associated with GPT involvement [4,27]. On the other hand, managers would incur monitoring costs or need to offer incentives for the analysts to disclose their GPT use if they benefit from such information. In sum, information asymmetry in analysts' GPT usage, or its reduction, suggests a potential shift in the incentives for GPT adoption among the manager-analyst dyad. In this section, we investigate the incentives for managers and analysts to adopt GPT and how these align with variations in the disclosure policy.

We gauge analysts' incentives for adopting GPT by their managers' quality evaluations of the research briefs and the perceived effort exerted (in hours) in creating them. We generalize the evaluations (either perceived quality or exerted effort) from manager i of deck version v ($v \in \{No-GPT, Human-GPT\}$) for RFP case c ($c \in \{1, 2, 3, 4\}$) as $Y_{i,c,v}$. We quantify analysts' interest in adopting GPT in Eq. 1 where the focal explanatory variable is Human-GPT$_{c,v}$ (coded as 1 for the Human-GPT deck and 0 for the No-GPT deck given an RFP c) and its interaction with Disclosure$_i$ (coded as 1 for the disclosure and 0 for the non-disclosure experimental condition). We include RFP case fixed effects η_c to account for any observed and unobserved heterogeneity in the evaluation stemming from the time-invariant features across the four RFP cases. We also account for manager-level heterogeneity by including manager-level fixed effects

γ_i in the specification, which absorb variations of the Disclosure$_i$ main effect. According to this specification, a positive (negative) coefficient estimate of β_1 indicates that analysts would receive better (worse, respectively) evaluations and greater (less, respectively) perceived effort by the managers' assessment of the Human-GPT versus the No-GPT deck under the non-disclosure policy. It is important to recognize that, as managers cannot identify the actual content generation source, β_1 accurately reflects the changes in analysts' performance or effort as perceived by the managers when utilizing GPT for research briefs. β_2 measures the impact of the disclosure policy against the non-disclosure policy on changes in evaluation: a positive (negative) coefficient suggests an increase (decrease, respectively) in the evaluation gain or loss from analysts' use of GPT to create the decks under the disclosure policy relative to the non-disclosure policy. Finally, the combined effect of β_1 and β_2 reflects the increase or decrease in managers' evaluations of a Human-GPT deck relative to the No-GPT deck under the disclosure policy, suggesting greater or less incentive for the analyst to use GPT under an enforced disclosure policy.

$$\begin{aligned} Y_{i,c,v} = \beta_0 + &\\ &\beta_1 \times \text{Human-GPT}_{c,v} + \\ &\beta_2 \times \text{Human-GPT}_{c,v} \times \text{Disclosure}_i + \\ &\eta_c + \gamma_i + \epsilon_{i,c,v} \end{aligned} \tag{1}$$

We measure manager i's incentive to adopt GPT by their stated preference to authorize analysts to use GPT for each content section s of a research brief SecGPTAuth$_{i,s}$ after evaluating the research briefs with or without the disclosure policy. Following the literature in the technology acceptance model [2,12,47], we specify in Eq. 2 a manager i's preference in authorizing GPT use influenced by the perceived usefulness (IndGPTUsefulness$_i$) and risk (IndGPTRisk$_i$) of GPT (both mean-centered) in contributing to the research brief. Managers' perceived risk of GPT use is measured by the average perception of misinformation raised from GPT responses and confidentiality breaches during analysts' interaction with GPT. We note that although managers perceived GPT as useful ($M_{Non-Disclosure} = 5.09$, $M_{Disclosure} = 5.07$, $p = 0.91$ given a two-sample Student's t-test) on a 7-point scale, managers state significant risk that GPT could potentially bring to content generation ($M_{Non-Disclosure} = 4.58$, $M_{Disclosure} = 4.56$, $p = 0.82$ given a two-sample Student's t-test) on a 5-point scale. We include research brief section-fixed effects γ_s to account for any observed and unobserved heterogeneity in the tendency to authorize analysts' GPT use across the research brief content sections. We account for manager-level heterogeneity by including manager-level controls X_i, which compromise the manager's gender, working hours per week, whether their work faces clients, whether they evaluated the No-GPT before the Human-GPT deck, and tenure as a consultant. According to the specification in Eq. 2, the coefficient estimates of γ_1 and γ_2 indicate how the perceived risk and usefulness influence managers' preference to adopt GPT under the non-disclosure policy. The coefficient estimate of γ_3 suggests managers' preference to adopt GPT under disclosure relative to the non-disclosure policy. Notably, the coefficient estimates of γ_4 and γ_5 measure the influence of the disclosure policy compared to the non-disclosure policy on shifts in managers' preference to adopt GPT driven by its perceived usefulness and associated risk. Consequently, the joint impact of γ_1, γ_3, and γ_4 shows how the perceived GPT risk affects managers' preference to adopt GPT under the disclosure policy; similarly, the combined influence of γ_2, γ_3, and γ_5 highlights how the perceived usefulness of GPT affects managers' preference to adopt it under the same disclosure policy.

$$
\begin{aligned}
\text{SecGPTAuth}_{i,s} = \gamma_0 + & \\
& \gamma_1 \times \text{IndGPTRisk}_i + \\
& \gamma_2 \times \text{IndGPTUsefulness}_i + \\
& \gamma_3 \times \text{Disclosure}_i + \\
& \gamma_4 \times \text{IndGPTRisk}_i \times \text{Disclosure}_i + \\
& \gamma_5 \times \text{IndGPTUsefulness}_i \times \text{Disclosure}_i + \\
& \gamma_6 \times X_i + \gamma_s + \epsilon_{i,s}
\end{aligned}
\tag{2}
$$

We consider managers and analysts share aligned incentives to adopt GPT when analysts are likely to receive better evaluations or be recognized for their greater effort by the managers in creating content for the Human-GPT deck compared to the No-GPT deck, while the managers would not forbid the analysts' GPT use. Importantly, we investigate how the alignment in the preference to adopt GPT varies when changing the disclosure policy. In particular, the consistent direction in the coefficient estimates for β_2, γ_4, and γ_5 implies a stronger alignment among the manager-analyst dyad in using GPT when enforcing a disclosure policy.

We apply the ordinary least square (OLS) estimation with robust standard errors clustered at the individual manager level for all analyses to allow for arbitrary error correlations within each manager. Table 2 presents the results. In particular, Columns (1) and (2) show the results related to analysts' incentive to adopt GPT by using managers' deck evaluation and effort estimation as the dependent variable following the specification shown in Eq. 1; Column (3) shows the results about managers' preference to adopt GPT according to the specification in Eq. 2. In the following sections, we interpret the results separately under the non-disclosure and disclosure conditions.

3.3 Non-disclosure Policy

We first investigate analysts' and managers' incentives in adopting GPT under the non-disclosure condition, the status quo, where the content generation source is obscured from the managers.

For the analysts, the positive and statistically significant coefficient estimate of β_1 in Table 2 Column (1) indicates that analysts benefit from using GPT to produce a research brief, as they receive better-quality evaluations from their superiors without disclosing its use. However, based on the coefficient estimate of β_1 in Table 2 Column (2), we do not find that managers consider generating this better content to require more significant effort from the analysts.

For the managers, the positive and statistically significant coefficient estimate of γ_2 in Table 2 Column (3) suggests that higher perceived usefulness of GPT increases managers' preference to authorize analysts' GPT use. However, the negative and statistically significant coefficient estimate of γ_1 in Table 2 Column (3) indicates that a higher perceived risk stemming from using GPT decreases managers' incentives to authorize the use of GPT. Since $IndGPTRisk$ and $IndGPTUsefulness$ are mean-centered, managers' average tendency to adopt GPT is 2.309 (coefficient estimate of γ_0), which is marginally statistically significant below the mid-point indicating adoption difference of the 5-point scale ($p = 0.05$ given a Z-test). Although managers considering GPT to be more useful (one standard deviation above the sample mean) do not show a significant preference for forbidding analysts' GPT use ($p = 0.97$ given a Z-test compared to the mid-point indicating adopting indifference), managers who hold greater risk concerns (one standard deviation above the sample mean) strongly forbid analysts' GPT use ($p < 0.01$ given a Z-test compared to the mid-point indicating adopting indifference).

The findings suggest that analysts could benefit from using GPT without disclosing it, as this could lead to better performance evaluations from their superiors. However, managers do not show a general positive tendency to adopt GPT, unless they consider GPT beneficial or at less risk of generating misinformation or confidentiality breaches when they do not know whether the analysts used GPT. Although a non-disclosure policy could encourage analysts' adoption, their superior would not authorize its use at large, leading to misaligned incentives in adopting GPT among the manager-analyst dyad. These findings corroborate the existing literature showing that GPT adoption frictions are primarily caused by the reservations of superiors [28] and explain why subordinates exhibit shadow adoption of GPT when enterprise-wide adoption is not implemented.

3.4 Disclosure Policy

We next investigate the incentives of analysts and managers adopting GPT under the disclosure condition where the content generation source is communicated to the managers.

The results shown in Table 2 Columns (1) suggest that analysts do not necessarily receive significantly worse evaluations from the managers when disclosing the GPT use for the Human-GPT deck given the non-statistically significant coefficient estimate of β_2. However, the advantage of the better-evaluated Human-GPT versus the No-GPT decks disappeared, as the combined coefficient estimate of β_1 and β_2 is not statistically different from zero ($p = 0.17$ given a Z-test). Notably, the negative statistically significant coefficient estimate of β_2 shown in Table 2 Column (2) suggests that managers perceive analysts to put in less effort in creating the Human-GPT deck when GPT use is disclosed compared to the No-GPT deck.

Table 2. The Impact of Disclosure on Manager-Analyst Incentives to Adopt GPT

	DV: DeckQuality (1)	DV: log(DeckHour) (2)	DV: SecGPTAuth (3)
Human-GPT (vs. No-GPT)	0.389***	0.079	
	(0.127)	(0.053)	
Human-GPT (vs. No-GPT) × Disclosure	−0.219	−0.387***	
	(0.182)	(0.091)	
IndGPTRisk			−0.514***
			(0.156)
IndGPTUsefulness			0.517***
			(0.107)
IndGPTRisk × Disclosure			0.549**
			(0.273)
IndGPTUsefulness × Disclosure			−0.226
			(0.137)
Disclosure			0.102
			(0.153)
Constant	3.992***	2.286***	2.309***
	(0.046)	(0.023)	(0.354)
Observations	238	238	552
Individual fixed-effects	Yes	Yes	No
Case fixed-effects	Yes	Yes	No
Pitch section fixed-effects	No	No	Yes
Individual controls	No	No	Yes

Notes: Standard errors in the parentheses are clustered at the individual manager level. * $p < 0.10$, ** $p < 0.05$, *** $p < 0.01$.

For the managers, the results shown in Table 2 Column (3) suggest: 1) the disclosure policy does not positively encourage managers to adopt GPT given the non-significant coefficient estimate of γ_3, and 2) the positive and statistically significant coefficient estimates of γ_4 suggest that an enforced disclosure policy could reduce the negative impact of risk concerns on managers' preferences to authorize the GPT use under the non-disclosure policy. In particular, managers with greater risk concerns (one standard deviation above the sample mean) do not show a significant preference for forbidding analysts' GPT use ($p = 0.14$ given a Z-test compared to the mid-point indicating adopting indifference). Importantly, our findings indicate that the enforced disclosure policy does not necessarily alleviate the broader misaligned interests between managers and analysts in utilizing GPT under a non-disclosure agreement. This conclusion is supported by the inconsistent signs in the coefficient estimates of β_2 and γ_4, as presented in Table 2, Columns (2) and (3).

In conclusion, the findings indicate that analysts might forfeit the advantages of GPT in enhancing content evaluation if they reveal their use to managers. In particular, the performance gain from using GPT has vanished compared to instances of non-disclosure, accompanied by less effort attributed to their content generation. On the other hand, our results suggest that an enforced disclosure policy could reduce the negative impact of managers' concerns about GPT risks on their incentive to adopt GPT when no such policy exists. This finding underscores the conflicting incentives for managers and analysts regarding GPT adoption, which a disclosure policy does not resolve.

3.5 Discussion

Our survey experiment results suggest that GPT has the potential to enhance content quality for professional service firms, aligning with existing research [39]. However, the successful integration of GPT in the workplace depends on aligned incentives for adoption and accountability in risk management, as seen through the lens of agency theory. To our knowledge, we are the first to demonstrate empirically that achieving such alignment poses significant challenges in a professional service firm, which adds to the well-documented friction surrounding GPT adoption across industries [28].

Professional service firms without an explicit GPT adoption and reinforced disclosure policy are subject to potential agency costs due to information asymmetry that managers cannot tell analysts' GPT use. In this case, firms cannot harness the benefits of analysts adopting GPT in content generation due to managers' hesitance to allow its use stemming from risk concerns about GPT's contribution to misinformation and confidentiality breaches. As a result, the information asymmetry in analysts' GPT uses implies a potential increase in monitoring costs and exacerbates the incentive misalignment in the manager-analyst dyad in enterprise-wide GPT adoption.

Although our results suggest an enforced disclosure policy would reduce the information asymmetry that causes the potential monitoring cost mentioned above, this policy alone would not reduce the misalignment in the incentives between managers and analysts in adopting GPT. On the one hand, the reinforcement in the disclosure policy could encourage managers' incentives to adopt GPT by reducing the negative impact of the risk concerns. On the other hand, the enforced disclosure policy makes analysts less likely to use GPT because managers tend to undervalue the performance and effort put in by analysts when knowing their GPT use. In professional service organizations, when the effort is undervalued, it suggests that managers have an inflated view of analysts' capacities, resulting in an anticipated reduction in analysts' hourly wages without improved performance assessments. Furthermore, the misaligned incentives in GPT adoption between managers and agents could be further worsened if analysts are also made accountable for any misinformation or confidentiality breaches when they disclose its use. The implications suggest that implementing a disclosure policy should be further accompanied by corporate AI policies that address accountability in risk-sharing and updated salary schemes related to GPT integration in the workplace.

4 Potential Solutions to Better Align Incentives of the Manager-Analyst Dyad in GPT Adoption

We have so far identified a general trend of misaligned incentives regarding the adoption of GPT among the manager-agent dyad, which points to a broader dilemma in GPT adoption with and without a disclosure policy. However, our empirical investigation does not fully explore whether some managers share a more aligned preference with an analyst in utilizing GPT. This could offer a preliminary solution and recommendation for a corporate AI policy, which we will discuss in this section.

4.1 Impact of Managers' Acknowledgment on Human Effort in the Alignment of GPT Adoption Among the Manager-Analyst Dyad

The findings from the previous section indicate that misalignment incentives between managers and analysts regarding the use of GPT occur in two ways: first, in situations lacking a disclosure policy, managers are reluctant to embrace GPT due to risk apprehensions. Second, with a disclosure policy in place, managers often underestimate analysts' performance and the effort required to prepare research briefs involving GPT. These situations highlight that for GPT to be effectively integrated into the manager-analyst dynamic, managers should recognize the human effort in content creation and allow the use of GPT, even amid significant risk concerns. Consequently, we focus on a specific group of managers who value analysts' efforts when utilizing GPT. This group usually possesses a more realistic view of their employees' abilities, which aids in maintaining analysts' hourly wages by controlling the number of tasks assigned in a given period. While safeguarding analysts' income, we also evaluate whether these managers have a favorable opinion of their subordinates' performance. Additionally, we explore if implementing a disclosure policy could help mitigate the negative impacts of risk on allowing analysts' GPT use.

We consider managers who would maintain their subordinates' workload when utilizing GPT if the relative estimated number of hours used to generate the Human-GPT is not less than that of the No-GPT deck for the same RFP case. Furthermore, we do not view managers as realistic if they consider a deck that requires less than four hours of work since the actual time spent generating a deck is approximately four hours without GPT. Table 3 Column (1) shows the subsample results related to analysts' incentive to adopt GPT by using managers' deck evaluation using the exact specification as shown in Table 2 Column (1).[2] Table 3 Column (2) shows the results regarding the same subgroup of managers' preference to adopt GPT according to the exact specification as in Table 2 Column (3).

[2] We do not investigate analysts' incentive to use GPT by managers' effort estimation since managers in this subgroup do not discount analysts' efforts in developing the decks.

We first investigate analysts' and managers' incentives for adopting GPT under the non-disclosure policy. For the analysts, the positive and statistically significant coefficient estimate of β_1 in Table 3 Column (1) indicates that analysts benefit from using GPT to produce a research brief. For the managers, their average tendency to adopt GPT is 2.569 (coefficient estimate of γ_0), which is not statistically significant below the mid-point indicating adoption difference of the 5-point scale ($p = 0.44$ given a Z-test), suggesting no significant preference to forbid analysts' GPT use. Consistent with the results shown in Table 2 Column (3), the positive and statistically significant coefficient estimate of γ_2 in Table 3 Column (2) suggests that a higher perceived usefulness of GPT increases managers' preference to authorize analysts' GPT use. The negative and statistically significant coefficient estimate of γ_1 in Table 3 Column (2) indicates that a higher perceived risk stemming from the use of GPT decreases managers' incentives to authorize the use of GPT. Managers contemplating the risks associated with GPT, defined as one standard deviation above the average, exhibit a marginally statistically significant tendency to prohibit analysts from using GPT ($p = 0.10$, based on a Z-test compared to the mid-point that suggests a stance of indifference). In summary, managers who acknowledge the importance of human effort in creating the Human-GPT, as opposed to the No-GPT deck without a disclosure policy, not only see improved performance but also would not forbid GPT usage unless they identify significant risks.

We next investigate analysts' and managers' incentives for adopting GPT under the disclosure policy. The findings in Table 3, Columns (1), indicate that analysts do not appear to be evaluated significantly worse by managers when revealing GPT use for the Human-GPT deck, as evidenced by the non-statistically significant coefficient estimate of β_2. However, the advantage of the better-evaluated Human-GPT compared to the No-GPT decks disappeared, as the combined coefficient estimate of β_1 and β_2 is not statistically different from zero ($p = 0.85$ based on a Z-test). For managers, the outcomes displayed in Table 3 Column (2) indicate that implementing a disclosure policy might lessen the adverse effect of risk concerns on their willingness to approve GPT usage under the non-disclosure policy, as evidenced by the positive and statistically significant coefficient estimates of γ_4. Specifically, managers with heightened risk concerns (one standard deviation above the sample mean) exhibit no significant preference against prohibiting analysts' use of GPT ($p = 0.74$ following a Z-test compared to the mid-point, suggesting a stance of indifference). Consequently, even though managers permitted their subordinates to utilize GPT under the disclosure policy, the previously recognized enhancement in performance of the Human-GPT compared to the No-GPT deck under the non-disclosure policy vanished. This suggests a misalignment of incentives within the manager-analysts relationship regarding the GPT adoption, despite managers not undermining analysts' efforts.

Table 3. The Impact of Disclosure on Manager-Analyst Incentives to Adopt GPTâĂŞ-Subsample Analysis When Managers Do Not Discount Effort When Analysts Used GPT

	DV: Quality (1)	DV: SecGPTAuth (2)
Human-GPT (vs. No-GPT)	0.437***	
	(0.156)	
Human-GPT (vs. No-GPT) × Disclosure	−0.403	
	(0.243)	
IndGPTRisk		−0.772***
		(0.210)
IndGPTUsefulness		0.578***
		(0.151)
IndGPTRisk × Disclosure		1.056***
		(0.339)
IndGPTUsefulness × Disclosure		−0.209
		(0.197)
Disclosure		0.440**
		(0.209)
Constant	4.213***	2.569***
	(0.060)	(0.558)
Observations	146	246
Individual fixed-effects	Yes	No
Case fixed-effects	Yes	No
Pitch section fixed-effects	No	Yes
Individual controls	No	Yes

Notes: Standard errors in the parentheses are clustered at the individual manager level. * $p < 0.10$, ** $p < 0.05$, *** $p < 0.01$.

4.2 Impact of Managers' Experience on the Alignment in GPT Adoption Among the Manager-Analyst Dyad Under the Disclosure Policy

Managers and their analysts show an alignment in incentives to use GPT within the non-disclosure policy when the managers acknowledge the effort put in by analysts in creating the Human-GPT deck. However, this optimism is still undermined by the disclosure policy, largely influenced by managers' diminished assessment of content generation quality due to analysts' use of GPT. This leads us to investigate whether differences exist among managers in their evaluations of the Human-GPT versus No-GPT presentations and their preference to allow GPT utilization. Previous studies indicate that managers' experience influences their willingness to embrace AI and its output [13,33,39,40]. We aim to empirically assess how the incentives for adopting GPT align between managers and analysts based on the managers' experience level under the disclosure policy. We concentrate on the disclosure condition of the subsample analyzed in Table 3 and exclude observations from the non-disclosure condition. Keep in mind that excluding these non-disclosure observations alters the specification, as indicated by Eqs. 1 and 2, since it removes terms associated with *Disclosure*.

To measure analysts' incentive to use GPT, we incorporate managers' experience through an interaction term between IndExperience (mean-centered) and Human-GPT. This enables us to examine how variations in managers' experience affect their assessments of content quality in the decks prepared by the analysts.[3] The OLS regression results are shown in Table 4 Column (1). Although managers, on average, do not recognize the improved quality of the Human-GPT (vs. No-GPT) deck, more experienced managers significantly value the Human-GPT deck compared to less experienced managers, given the positive and statistically significant coefficient estimate of the interaction term between Human-GPT and IndExperience. Moreover, more experienced managers (one standard deviation above the mean) significantly prefer the Human-GPT deck over the No-GPT deck ($p < 0.05$ based on a Z-test). In contrast, this favorable assessment is absent among less experienced managers ($p = 0.12$ according to a Z-test).

To measure managers' incentive to adopt GPT, we introduce IndExperience and its interaction with IndGPTRisk and IndGPTUsefulness to understand whether managers' experience would change their tendency to allow GPT use. The results are shown in Table 4 Column (2). On average, managers do not exhibit a notable preference against allowing analysts to use GPT. This conclusion stems from the constant term's coefficient estimate of 3.171, which is not statistically significant under the midpoint of the 5-point scale ($p = 0.79$ from a Z-test). While more experienced managers show greater awareness of the risks associated with adopting GPT for analysts, they also perceive greater benefits in using GPT compared to their less experienced counterparts. We observe that managers, regardless of their experience level, do not significantly favor banning analysts' GPT ($ps > 0.85$ as indicated by Z-tests to the preference midpoint, implying a neutral position).

In conclusion, managers with more experience who value analysts' contributions in utilizing GPT for content creation help reduce the misaligned incentives in GPT adoption between the manager-agent relationship under the disclosure policy.

[3] The primary influence of IndExperience is captured by the individual-level fixed effects.

Table 4. The Impact of Managers' Experience on Manager-Analyst Incentives to Adopt GPT under the Disclosure Policy

	DV: Quality	DV: SecGPTAuth
	(1)	(2)
Human-GPT (vs. No-GPT)	0.013	
	(0.156)	
Human-GPT (vs. No-GPT) × IndExperience	0.362**	
	(0.148)	
IndGPTRisk		−0.563
		(0.376)
IndGPTUsefulness		0.235
		(0.214)
IndGPTRisk × IndExperience		−0.984**
		(0.394)
IndGPTUsefulness × IndExperience		0.202**
		(0.094)
IndExperience		0.490
		(0.385)
Constant	4.322***	3.171***
	(0.077)	(0.630)
Observations	58	114
Individual fixed-effects	Yes	No
Case fixed-effects	Yes	No
Pitch section fixed-effects	No	Yes
Individual controls	No	Yes

Notes: Standard errors in the parentheses are clustered at the individual manager level. * $p < 0.10$, ** $p < 0.05$, *** $p < 0.01$.

4.3 Discussion

Although the primary findings from Sect. 3 indicate a misalignment between managers and analysts in adopting GPT, this section explores specific groups of managers who improve alignment within the manager-analyst relationship regarding GPT adoption. Specifically, our findings indicate that managers who do not diminish the significance of human effort exerted in content generation could perceive that analysts perform better when GPT is employed, depending on either a non-disclosure policy or a disclosure policy restricted to more experienced managers. These findings indicate that professional service firms should focus on identifying experienced managers who do not overlook the efforts of their subordinates when using GPT. This method proves advantageous when corporate AI policies are lacking. Specifically, a company can gain productivity through GPT integration while concurrently developing and enacting AI policies that clarify risk-sharing responsibilities and introduce revised salary frameworks associated with GPT implementation in the workplace.

Our findings advance the emerging literature on GPT adoption [7,13,39]. While prior studies indicate that less experienced consulting workers might have greater incentives to adopt GPT [13], our results imply that this adoption strategy may be inefficient in a manager-analyst dynamic, especially if consulting workers hold managerial roles. We also highlight the significance of experienced managers within consulting firms. Although they may not gain the most immediate benefits from directly using GPT, they tend to support their subordinates' use of GPT when they recognize its advantages. Furthermore, we observe that the disclosure policy fosters this alignment of interests while managers still account for the hours analysts spend creating the deck using GPT, pointing to a need for policies that ensure managers objectively acknowledge analysts' contributions when leveraging GPT.

5 Conclusions

The empirical results highlight novel dilemmas associated with information asymmetry and moral hazard that may arise from subordinates' adoption of ChatGPT in consulting firms. We specifically identified how these agency problems affect the adoption of ChatGPT and the management of risks associated with misinformation and confidentiality. Agency scholarship identifies multiple solutions to address agency problems in firms, including the adoption of monitoring mechanisms and incentive structures [20], as well as the implementation of cooperation strategies between individuals and teams [35]. While specific actions based on these solutions are certainly needed, the question remains regarding the appropriate instruments to implement and formalize this wide array of solutions [6].

We suggest that the adoption of AI corporate policies is the most effective means to address these agency problems for multiple reasons. First, the absence of a corporate-wide policy would result in agency problems arising from the individual use of ChatGPT being handled on a case-by-case basis, exposing the firm to multiple and diverse risks associated with each single solution and adding friction to ChatGPT adoption. Second, the implementation of an AI corporate policy introduces a contractual component within the firm, whereby the duties between principals and agents related to the use of ChatGPT and other generative AI software become part of the "agency law within the corporation." This means that agents within the firm will be explicitly bound through a contractual duty to the principal, aligning both parties in terms of information sharing and responsibilities. Finally, an AI corporate policy ensures that risks are shared and known to both principals and agents, aligning the adoption of ChatGPT not only with the interests of managers but also with the broader interests of the firm.

We propose that an AI corporate policy should encompass at least four key elements to effectively address agency problems resulting from the agents' use of ChatGPT. First, the policy should mandate a disclosure obligation requiring agents to inform principals whenever they use ChatGPT for task completion. This transparency reduces information asymmetry, enabling managers to request and access the necessary information to assess the quality and authenticity of the work produced, and implement appropriate controls to mitigate risks associated with misinformation and confidentiality breaches. Second, the policy should establish a risk-sharing framework to align the interests of both principals and agents. By formally incorporating the use of ChatGPT or similar tools into the contractual duties of employees, both principals and agents are aware of their shared responsibilities and accountabilities, addressing moral hazard by ensuring agents are not incentivized to take undue risks, such as improperly sharing confidential information or over-relying on AI-generated content without oversight. Third, a monitoring mechanism should be implemented to ensure agents respect their duties. This mechanism should allow for the verification of whether agents disclose ChatGPT use, assess the types of risks agents incur by using ChatGPT, and review the actual outputs produced with ChatGPT to avoid legal issues such as misrepresentation and copyright violations. Finally, an incentive mechanism should be implemented to acknowledge the work done by agents with the help of ChatGPT without discounting their effort. This mechanism is necessary to align the interests of agents using ChatGPT with those of the principals in serving clients effectively.

This approach to corporate AI policy includes tracking ChatGPT usage, which would incur agency costs for managers. However, it embodies the intra-corporate duty of candor, as advocated by Langevoort, which imposes an affirmative duty on employees to disclose relevant information. Furthermore, we believe that monitoring ChatGPT use is essential to prevent diminished work quality and inadequate risk management. The Hamburg Labor Court case illustrates that simply authorizing the use of ChatGPT does not constitute a comprehensive policy, nor does it grant employers oversight of employee usage. Despite having AI guidelines and a handbook, the company remained unaware of ChatGPT adoption, revealing a critical gap in management's visibility. These findings underscore the importance of disclosure, aligning with regulatory frameworks such as the AI Act (Regulation (EU) 2024/1689), which requires providers and deployers of AI systems to ensure their staff and other individuals involved in the operation and use of AI systems have sufficient AI literacy (Article 4). This obligation came into effect on February 2, 2025. At present, it remains unclear whether employers will be considered "deployers" when they simply allow employees to use freely accessible AI systems, such as ChatGPT. However, this qualification is certainly possible, particularly if employers implement specific GPT use policies. Furthermore, employers could also be considered "providers" of AI systems if they customize GPT-based AI systems for internal use. Consequently, we believe that employers, as part of their AI literacy initiatives, should pay special attention to disclosure and the responsible use of AI. Consistent with existing literature, our analysis reaffirms that disclosure is an effective mechanism for addressing misalignment of interests in the workplace. The rise of generative AI presents a timely opportunity to strengthen this principle.

Acknowledgments. This research was supported by funding from HEC Paris. The authors also thank colleagues at HEC Paris for their helpful comments and advice, which contributed to improving this work.

Disclosure of Interests. The authors have no competing interests to declare that are relevant to the content of this article.

Appendix

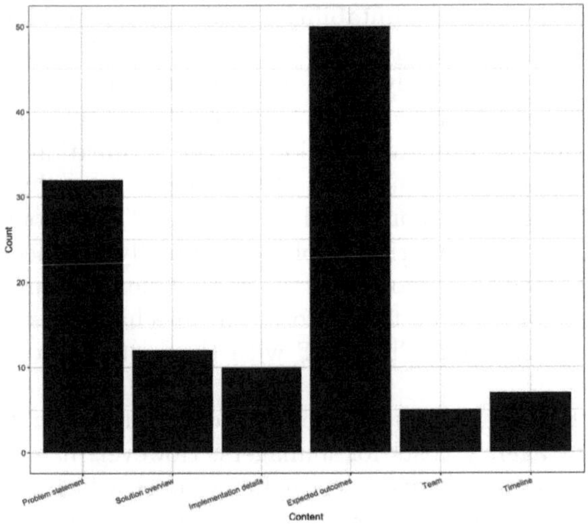

Fig. 5. Number of prompts used in each content generation section.

Table 5. Items used to measure the constructs

Construct	Item
DeckQuality	1. The problem description is accurate and clear.
	2. The content is highly informative.
	3. The proposed solutions are feasible.
IndGPTUsefulness	1. How useful is ChatGPT for generating a research brief given the summarizing prompts?
	2. How useful is ChatGPT for generating a research brief given the inferring prompts?
	3. How useful is ChatGPT for generating a research brief given the text transforming prompts?
	4. How useful is ChatGPT for generating a research brief given the expanding prompts?
IndGPTRisk	1. Do you worry about misinformation generated by ChatGPT for your work?
	2. Are you concerned about confidentiality issues related to content input into ChatGPT for your work?

Table 6. Variable name and definition

Variable Name	Explanation
Individual-level Variables	
IndGPTUsefulness	An individual manager's perceived usefulness of GPT in generating a research brief. This index is the average of the four items shown in Table 5.
IndGPTRisk	An individual manager's perceived riskiness of GPT in generating a research brief. This index is the average of the two items shown in Table 5.
IndFemale	Whether an individual manager is female.
IndWeekWorkingHour	The average number of hours an individual manager worked per week (level 1: less than 45 h; level 2: less than 50 h; level 3: less than 60 h; level 4: other).
IndTenure	The tenure of an individual manager in consulting (level 1: less than a year; level 2: one to five years; level 3: five to seven years; level 4: more than 7 years).
IndNoGPTDeckFirst	Whether an individual manager evaluated a No-GPT deck before evaluating a Human-GPT deck.
IndClientFacing	Whether an individual manager has a client-facing role.
IndExperience	The familiarity with the RFP process on a scale from one to five. We take the average of the familiarity of the RFP process across the two evaluated cases for managers recruited from the first wave of data collection.
Individual-case-deck-level Variables	
DeckQuality	An individual manager's perceived deck quality (No-GPT or human-GPT) given a case. The index is an average of four items shown in Table 5.
DeckHour	The perceived number of hours used to generate a deck (No-GPT or human-GPT) given a certain case.
Individual-case section-level Variables	
SecGPTAuth	The likelihood of an individual manager allowing the analysts to use GPT to prepare business content on a scale from one to five.

References

1. 24 BVGa 1/24
2. Agarwal, R., Prasad, J.: A conceptual and operational definition of personal innovativeness in the domain of information technology. Inf. Syst. Res. **9**(2), 204–215 (1998)
3. Bergen, M., Dutta, S., Walker, O.C., Jr.: Agency relationships in marketing: a review of the implications and applications of agency and related theories. J. Mark. **56**(3), 1–24 (1992)
4. Bosse, D.A., Phillips, R.A.: Agency theory and bounded self-interest. Acad. Manag. Rev. **41**(2), 276–297 (2016)
5. Bratton, W.: Thenexus of contracts' corporation: a critical appraisal. Cornell Law Rev. **74**, 407 (1989)
6. Brudney, V.: Contract and fiduciary duty in corporate law. BCL Rev. **38**, 595 (1996)
7. Brynjolfsson, E., Li, D., Raymond, L.R.: Generative AI at work. Technical report, National Bureau of Economic Research (2023)
8. Castelo, N., Bos, M.W., Lehmann, D.: Let the machine decide: when consumers trust or distrust algorithms. NIM Marketing Intell. Rev. **11**(2), 24–29 (2019)
9. Charfeddine, M., Kammoun, H.M., Hamdaoui, B., Guizani, M.: ChatGPT's security risks and benefits: offensive and defensive use-cases, mitigation measures, and future implications. IEEE Access (2024)

10. Chiu, I.H.Y., Lim, E.W.: Managing corporations' risk in adopting artificial intelligence: a corporate responsibility paradigm. Wash. U. Global Stud. L. Rev. **20**, 347 (2021)
11. Crothers, E.N., Japkowicz, N., Viktor, H.L.: Machine-generated text: a comprehensive survey of threat models and detection methods. IEEE Access **11**, 70977–71002 (2023)
12. Davis, F.D.: Perceived usefulness, perceived ease of use, and user acceptance of information technology. MIS Quart. 319–340 (1989)
13. Dell'Acqua, F., et al.: Navigating the jagged technological frontier: field experimental evidence of the effects of AI on knowledge worker productivity and quality. SSRN Electron. J. (2023)
14. Devlin, J., Chang, M.W., Lee, K., Toutanova, K.: Bert: pre-training of deep bidirectional transformers for language understanding. arXiv preprint arXiv:1810.04805 (2018)
15. Dietvorst, B.J., Simmons, J.P., Massey, C.: Algorithm aversion: people erroneously avoid algorithms after seeing them err. J. Exp. Psychol. Gen. **144**(1), 114 (2015)
16. Dodge, J., Liao, Q.V., Zhang, Y., Bellamy, R.K., Dugan, C.: Explaining models: an empirical study of how explanations impact fairness judgment. In: International Conference on Intelligent User Interfaces (2019)
17. Dou, Y., Forbes, M., Koncel-Kedziorski, R., Smith, N.A., Choi, Y.: Is GPT-3 text indistinguishable from human text? scarecrow: a framework for scrutinizing machine text. arXiv preprint arXiv:2107.01294 (2021)
18. Easterbrook, F.H., Fischel, D.R.: Corporate contract, the Colum. L. Rev. **89**, 1416 (1989)
19. Eisenhardt, K.M.: Agency-and institutional-theory explanations: the case of retail sales compensation. Acad. Manag. J. **31**(3), 488–511 (1988)
20. Eisenhardt, K.M.: Agency theory: an assessment and review. Acad. Manag. Rev. **14**(1), 57–74 (1989)
21. Falkner, A., Palomares, C., Franch, X., Schenner, G., Aznar, P., Schoerghuber, A.: Identifying requirements in requests for proposal: a research preview. In: Knauss, E., Goedicke, M. (eds.) REFSQ 2019. LNCS, vol. 11412, pp. 176–182. Springer, Cham (2019). https://doi.org/10.1007/978-3-030-15538-4_13
22. Fama, E.F.: Agency problems and the theory of the firm. J. Polit. Econ. **88**(2), 288–307 (1980)
23. Gibbons, R.: Incentives in organizations. J. Econ. Perspect. **12**(4), 115–132 (1998)
24. Gregor, S., Benbasat, I.: Explanations from intelligent systems: theoretical foundations and implications for practice. MIS Q. **23**(4), 497–530 (1999)
25. Gupta, M., Akiri, C., Aryal, K., Parker, E., Praharaj, L.: From chatGPT to threatGPT: impact of generative AI in cybersecurity and privacy. IEEE Access (2023)
26. Hacker, P., Engel, A., Mauer, M.: Regulating chatGPT and other large generative AI models. In: Proceedings of the 2023 ACM Conference on Fairness, Accountability, and Transparency, pp. 1112–1123 (2023)
27. Harris, M., Raviv, A.: Optimal incentive contracts with imperfect information. J. Econ. Theory **20**(2), 231–259 (1979)
28. Humlum, A., Vestergaard, E.: The adoption of chatGPT. University of Chicago, Becker Friedman Institute for Economics Working Paper (2024-50) (2024)
29. Jensen, M.C., Meckling, W.H.: Theory of the firm: managerial behavior, agency costs and ownership structure. J. Financ. Econ. **3**(4), 305–360 (1976)
30. Keeley, M.: Organizational analogy: a comparison of organismic and social contract models. Administ. Sci. Quart. 337–362 (1980)

31. Lage, I., et al.: Human evaluation of models built for interpretability. In: Proceedings of the AAAI Conference on Human Computation and Crowdsourcing, vol. 7, pp. 59–67 (2019)
32. Langevoort, D.C.: Managing the expectations gap in inventor protection: the sec and the post-enron reform agenda. Vill. L. Rev. **48**, 1139 (2003)
33. Logg, J.M., Minson, J.A., Moore, D.A.: Algorithm appreciation: people prefer algorithmic to human judgment. Organ. Behav. Hum. Decis. Process. **151**, 90–103 (2019)
34. Longoni, C., Bonezzi, A., Morewedge, C.K.: Resistance to medical artificial intelligence. J. Consumer Res. **46**(4), 629–650 (2019)
35. Miller, G.J.: Solutions to principal-agent problems in firms. In: Ménard, C., Shirley, M.M. (eds.) Handbook of new Institutional Economics, pp. 349–370. Springer, Heidelberg (2005). https://doi.org/10.1007/978-3-540-69305-5_15
36. Mills, P.A.: Agency, auditing and the unregulated environment: some further historical evidence. Account. Audit. Account. J. **3**(1), 0–0 (1990)
37. Mitchell, R., Meacheam, D.: Knowledge worker control: understanding via principal and agency theory. Learn. Organ. **18**(2), 149–160 (2011)
38. Ng, A., Fulford, I.: Deeplearningai: ChatGPT prompt engineering for developers (2023). https://www.deeplearning.ai/short-courses/chatgpt-prompt-engineering-for-developers/. Accessed 14 Jun 2023
39. Noy, S., Zhang, W.: Experimental evidence on the productivity effects of generative artificial intelligence. Science **381**(6654), 187–192 (2023). https://doi.org/10.1126/science.adh2586
40. Peng, Kalliamvakou, E., Cihon, P., Demirer, M.: The impact of AI on developer productivity: evidence from github copilot. arXiv preprint arXiv:2302.06590 (2023)
41. Poursabzi-Sangdeh, F., Goldstein, D.G., Hofman, J.M., Wortman Vaughan, J.W., Wallach, H.: Manipulating and measuring model interpretability. In: Proceedings of the 2021 CHI Conference on Human Factors in Computing Systems, pp. 1–52 (2021)
42. Rubin, J., Sheremeta, R.: Principal-agent settings with random shocks. Manage. Sci. **62**(4), 985–999 (2016)
43. Senoner, J., Netland, T., Feuerriegel, S.: Using explainable artificial intelligence to improve process quality: evidence from semiconductor manufacturing. Manag. Sci. **forthcoming** (2021)
44. Sharma, A.: Professional as agent: knowledge asymmetry in agency exchange. Acad. Manag. Rev. **22**(3), 758–798 (1997)
45. Shavell, S.: Risk sharing and incentives in the principal and agent relationship. Bell J. Econ. 55–73 (1979)
46. Spremann, K.: Agent and principal. In: Bamberg, G., Spremann, K. (eds.) Agency Theory, Information, and Incentives, pp. 3–37. Springer, Heidelberg (1987). https://doi.org/10.1007/978-3-642-75060-1_2
47. Venkatesh, V., Davis, F.D.: A theoretical extension of the technology acceptance model: four longitudinal field studies. Manage. Sci. **46**(2), 186–204 (2000)
48. Wang, W., Benbasat, I.: Recommendation agents for electronic commerce: effects of explanation facilities on trusting beliefs. J. Manag. Inf. Syst. **23**(4), 217–246 (2007)
49. You, S., Yang, C.L., Li, X.: Algorithmic versus human advice: does presenting prediction performance matter for algorithm appreciation? J. Manag. Inf. Syst. **39**(2), 336–365 (2022)
50. Zeckhauser, R.J., Pratt, J.W.: Principals and Agents: The Structure of Business. Harvard Business School Press, Boston (1985)

Author Index

© The Editor(s) (if applicable) and The Author(s), under exclusive license
to Springer Nature Switzerland AG 2026

D. Restrepo Amariles and K. Satoh (Eds.): *Compliance for Artificial Intelligence Systems*,
LNAI 14377, p. 127, 2026.
https://doi.org/10.1007/978-3-032-12795-2

MIX
Papier aus verantwortungsvollen Quellen
Paper from responsible sources
FSC® C105338

If you have any concerns about our products,
you can contact us on
ProductSafety@springernature.com

In case Publisher is established outside the EU,
the EU authorized representative is:
Springer Nature Customer Service Center GmbH
Europaplatz 3, 69115 Heidelberg, Germany

Printed by Libri Plureos GmbH
in Hamburg, Germany